Python for AI Cybersecurity: Defending World (2025 – 2030)

Building Cyber Defences with Python and AI: Hands-On Protection for Cloud, Blockchain, and IoT Systems

By Dr Israel Carlos Lomovasky

About the Book

Python for AI Cybersecurity: Defending the New Digital World (2025–2030)

 Master the Skills, Tools, and Strategies to Defend the Future — Today

---

Book Summary

In an era where cyberattacks grow smarter by the second and AI becomes both a weapon and a shield, *Python for AI Cybersecurity: Defending the New Digital World (2025–2030)* is your indispensable guide to mastering the next generation of cyber defence.

Whether you're a cybersecurity practitioner aiming to sharpen your skills, a Python programmer ready to level up into high-demand domains, or a tech visionary preparing for the next five years,
this book is your bridge into the real battlefield of AI-powered cybersecurity.

Real-world strategies
Comprehensive Python projects
Expertly explained AI models
Critical ethical insights
Forecasts for 2030 and beyond

No fluff. No hypothetical theory.
Only battle-ready knowledge and tools you can use right now.

Who Should Read This Book?

- Aspiring and current cybersecurity professionals

- Python developers eager to apply AI in security

- AI/ML practitioners entering the cybersecurity domain

- SOC analysts, threat hunters, red teamers, blue teamers

- Ethical hackers, penetration testers, and CISO strategists

- Students preparing for tomorrow's most lucrative and critical career paths

What You'll Learn:

Foundations of AI-driven cyber defence and offense
Building anomaly detectors, threat intelligence systems, smart contract auditors, IoT defenders, and more
Cutting-edge techniques: cloud-native security, blockchain threat modelling, adversarial AI defence
Tools mastery: Scikit-learn, TensorFlow, PyCaret, PyOD, Scapy, and dozens more
Real-world projects — fully coded and explained step-by-step
How to predict, prevent, and outpace zero-day threats with AI

Ethical frameworks to build trusted, responsible AI security solutions

---

What Makes This Book Different?

Ultra-practical: Every chapter delivers **hands-on, usable content** — not just concepts.

Fully updated for 2025–2030 realities: Covers quantum threats, autonomous SOCs, edge AI security, adversarial ML, and more.

For beginners-to-intermediate professionals: Explained clearly, progressively, without assuming advanced AI/ML knowledge at the start.

Ethical and future-ready: Every project and model is designed with legal compliance and ethical best practices in mind.

Complete guide: Introduction, foundational chapters, specialized deep dives, full project walkthroughs, appendices, further reading, and inspirational closure.

Praise for *Python for AI Cybersecurity*

"A masterclass in the real-world application of AI in cybersecurity. No fluff, just actionable intelligence."

"The only book I've seen that truly prepares security professionals for the autonomous, AI-driven future of threats."

"Accessible to beginners, rich enough for professionals. If you defend anything digital, you need this book."

Prepare to Defend the Future.

Get your copy of *Python for AI Cybersecurity: Defending the New Digital World (2025–2030)* today
Build real-world, career-changing skills
Step into the future fully armed with knowledge, strategy, ethics, and cutting-edge Python power

The world is changing.
The threats are changing.
Be ready.

Table of Contents

Python for AI Cybersecurity: Defending the New Digital World (2025–2030)

Preface

In the dawn of the 2025–2030 era, the digital landscape is more expansive — and more vulnerable — than ever before.

The unprecedented acceleration of artificial intelligence has reshaped not only industries and economies, but the very nature of security itself.

Today, **cybersecurity is no longer a purely human battle.** AI agents patrol, predict, defend, and sometimes attack — faster and smarter than any manual defender ever could.

The lines between attacker and defender are blurred.
The pace of threat evolution is relentless.
The stakes are nothing less than critical infrastructure, financial stability, public safety, and personal privacy.

This book was born from a simple but urgent realization:

Tomorrow's defenders must speak the language of AI fluently —

or they will be outpaced, outmaneuvered, and overwhelmed.

Why I Wrote This Book

There is an ocean of information about cybersecurity.
There is an ocean of information about artificial intelligence.
But very few guides exist that bridge these two critical worlds
— **practically, clearly, and completely.**

This book is designed to close that gap:

- Not just to explain what AI can do for cybersecurity — but to show you how.

- Not just to discuss futuristic ideas — but to empower you with **battle-ready skills** for 2025 and beyond.

- Not just to theorize — but to **build real-world Python systems** that can defend real assets.

Who This Book Is For

If you're an **aspiring cybersecurity professional** who wants to sharpen your edge,
A **Python developer** ready to leap into one of the fastest-growing, highest-paying domains,
A **seasoned analyst or engineer** preparing for AI-driven transformations in your SOC,
A **student, visionary, or innovator** who wants to defend the new digital world we are building,

— this book is for you.

You don't need a PhD in machine learning or years of coding experience to start.

You just need:

- Curiosity

- Determination

- A willingness to think creatively, act boldly, and adapt constantly

If you have those, you already belong among the next generation of cyber defenders.

What You Will Find Inside

 Foundational knowledge about how AI and cybersecurity intersect today — and how they are evolving through 2030 and beyond.
 Hands-on Python projects for anomaly detection, smart contract auditing, IoT security, cloud defence, blockchain fraud analysis, and more.
 Complete walkthroughs of AI models tailored for real cybersecurity applications.
 Advanced concepts like adversarial machine learning, autonomous defence, predictive risk modelling, and ethical AI governance.
 Future roadmaps to help you anticipate changes, prepare your career, and build sustainable, ethical AI systems.
 Bonus chapters (11,12) on the future of AI cyberwarfare, and the ethical and legal frameworks every responsible practitioner must embrace.

My Promise to You

- Every chapter is written to be **accessible** to those with basic Python skills and some cybersecurity knowledge.

- Every project is **real-world grounded** — not academic, not theoretical, but deployable.

- Every explanation is **clear, detailed, and practical**, respecting your time and ambition.

- Every future scenario is **bold, realistic, and built on current, cutting-edge trajectories**.

- Every model, strategy, and framework is presented **with ethics and responsibility at the core**.

A Final Word Before You Begin

The defenders of the 2025–2030 digital world are not passive.
They are not followers.
They are builders, leaders, guardians.

They are you — if you choose to be.

The skills you gain through these pages will not just defend companies or systems.
They will defend freedoms.
They will defend lives.
They will defend the foundations of the next civilization we are creating — one innovation at a time.

The mission is real.

The threats are real.

The future is real.

And it needs you.

Let's get to work.

Introduction: The New AI-Powered Cyber Arms Race

0.1 Welcome to a New Era of Cybersecurity

Imagine a world where a phishing email is not clumsily written, but crafted by an AI that knows your boss's tone, your work style, and the exact project you're stressed about.
Imagine malware that not only infects a machine but learns how its environment works and adapts its behavior automatically.
Imagine a security operations center powered by AI that triages millions of alerts, predicts threats before they happen, and even autonomously neutralizes attacks in real time.

Welcome to cybersecurity from **2025 onwards**.

This isn't science fiction.
This is **now** — and it's accelerating fast.

In today's digital world, **artificial intelligence (AI)** is **no longer optional** in cybersecurity.
It's the weapon of choice for attackers and the shield of hope for defenders.
It's changing how battles are fought — and who wins them.

This book exists because you, as a cybersecurity professional, cannot afford to be left behind.

0.2 The Critical Role of AI in Cybersecurity

For decades, cybersecurity relied heavily on **signatures**, **rules**, and **known behaviors**:

- Antivirus tools would match a malware file to a known virus database.

- Firewalls would block known malicious IP addresses.

- SIEMs (Security Information and Event Management) would raise alerts based on predefined thresholds.

But what happens when:

- The malware is brand new?

- The IP address rotates every second?

- The attacker mimics legitimate user behavior?

Rule-based systems fail.

Cyberattacks have evolved:

- They are now **faster**, **more sophisticated**, and **more automated** than ever.

- They adapt in **real-time**, learning from your defences.

Defenders must adapt too — and AI is the ultimate force multiplier.

AI in cybersecurity means **going beyond reacting** to attacks — it means **predicting, preventing, and neutralizing** them proactively.

0.3 Why Python?

You might wonder:

"Why is this book so focused on Python?"

Simple answer:

Python is the #1 programming language for cybersecurity AI development today.

It's not just "popular."
Python is the **industry standard** for:

- Building custom detection scripts
- Processing threat intelligence feeds
- Training machine learning models
- Deploying defensive tools into production

It's also:

- **Readable**: Easy to understand even for beginners
- **Powerful**: Supported by thousands of cybersecurity and AI libraries
- **Flexible**: Works across operating systems, servers, cloud platforms, and embedded devices

Whether you want to automate threat detection, build an anomaly detection model, or integrate AI into your SOC pipeline — **Python is your weapon of choice**.

This book will teach you **not just concepts** but **real coding skills**, step-by-step, **through fully explained practical examples**.

0.4 Who This Book Is For

This book was crafted with **you** in mind if you are:

- An aspiring cybersecurity professional with beginner-to-intermediate Python skills
- A SOC analyst, penetration tester, threat hunter, or red-teamer

- A security architect or engineer looking to add AI to your defences

- A self-taught hacker, coder, or cybersecurity enthusiast

- A student or career-changer wanting to leap ahead into the most future-proof security skills

You don't need to be a machine learning expert.
You don't need to be a senior programmer.

If you can read and write basic Python, this book will help you:

Understand how AI is used in real-world cybersecurity
Learn how to code your own defensive and offensive AI tools
Master the strategies that will shape cybersecurity from 2025–2030 and beyond

0.5 How This Book Is Structured

This book is designed as both a **roadmap** and a **toolkit** — guiding you step-by-step from foundational knowledge to cutting-edge real-world application.

You will find it carefully divided into **four major parts**, plus **two bonus chapters(11 and 12)**, **extensive appendices**, and an **inspirational epilogue** to forge your next steps as a cyber defender.

Part I: Foundations of AI Cybersecurity

In the first chapters, you will:

- Understand how artificial intelligence reshapes cybersecurity fundamentally.

- Explore both **offensive AI threats** and **defensive AI strategies**.

- Learn the core principles behind AI-powered threat intelligence and zero-day detection.

Goal: Build a solid, practical understanding of how AI transforms the cyber battlefield.

Part II: Applied Domains of AI Cybersecurity

We then dive into the most critical technological arenas:

- Defending **cloud infrastructure** with dynamic AI systems.

- Protecting **IoT ecosystems** and billions of devices in smart cities, industries, and homes.

- Securing **blockchain systems and smart contracts**, the new frontier of digital value transfer.

Goal: Master how AI specifically adapts to secure different, fast-evolving domains.

Part III: Tools, Platforms, and Practical Builds

You will then learn:

- The essential **Python libraries**, **frameworks**, and **platforms** powering modern AI cybersecurity.

- How to build your **first fully operational AI cybersecurity system**, step-by-step, using real Python code and best practices.

Goal: Move from concepts to creation — developing operational, real-world defensive systems.

Part IV: Strategic Futures and Ethical Imperatives

Finally, we prepare you for:

- The **future of cybersecurity in the 2030+ world** — from autonomous AI wars to quantum threats.

- The **ethical, legal, and human rights challenges** that cybersecurity AI professionals must address head-on.

Goal: Equip you not just to survive, but to **lead responsibly** in the next digital era.

Bonus Chapters (11 and 12)

Two deeply expanded bonus chapters provide:

- A strategic forecast of **AI cybersecurity through 2030 and beyond**.

- A critical guide to the **ethical and legal challenges** facing AI cybersecurity professionals worldwide.

Goal: Sharpen your strategic foresight and ethical decision-making capacity.

Appendices

Three powerful appendices offer:

- The best **open-source datasets** for building and testing cybersecurity AI models.

- A curated list of **project ideas** to expand your skills through practical challenges.

- An advanced guide to **additional Python tools** every defender must master.

Goal: Extend your learning with powerful real-world resources.

Epilogue

The closing section is an inspirational call to action:

- To step into your role as a leader and protector in the new AI-driven digital frontier.

- To use the skills you gain here **to safeguard not only systems, but lives, freedoms, and futures.**

How to Get the Most from This Book

You can read it linearly, building your knowledge progressively.

Or jump into specific parts — each chapter is designed to be **self-contained** and **highly actionable**.

The more you code, build, and test as you read, the faster and deeper your mastery will grow.

This is not a book you merely read.

It is a book you work with.
It is a book you transform yourself through.
It is a book you defend the future with.

0.6 The Real-World Focus of This Book

Unlike other books that stay theoretical, **this book is ruthlessly practical**.

You'll read about **real companies** using AI for security: (CrowdStrike, Darktrace, Microsoft, AWS, Google Cloud, and more).

 You'll see **actual strategies attackers use** (like AI-generated phishing and adversarial examples).

 You'll learn about **defences being deployed in 2025 and beyond**, including the use of LLMs, behavioral baselining, and autonomous security co-pilots.

 Every Python project is based on **real-world applications** — from anomaly detection on cloud logs to automating threat feed ingestion.

0.7 The Future Belongs to Cybersecurity Professionals Who Understand AI

By 2030:

- AI will **not just assist**, it will **lead** many cyber defences.

- SOC analysts will work **alongside AI co-pilots**.

- Offensive AI will create **new threat vectors** we haven't even imagined yet.

- Quantum computers will **break traditional cryptography**, forcing a complete rethink of cybersecurity strategies.

- "Human-in-the-loop" security systems will be the **default** — blending human expertise with AI speed and scalability.

Those who master Python and AI today will be the architects, leaders, and protectors of the digital world tomorrow.

This book is your gateway.

Chapter 1: Foundations — AI Meets Cybersecurity

1.1 The Evolving Threat Landscape (Expanded and Deeply Explained)

Cybersecurity: From Static Defences to Dynamic Battlegrounds

In the early 2000s, cybersecurity was largely a **signature-driven world**:

- Antivirus software updated virus signature databases daily.
- Intrusion Detection Systems (IDS) scanned for known malicious patterns.
- Firewalls blocked traffic based on predefined rulesets.

If an attacker reused a known malware or technique, they were blocked.
If they created something new — defenders were often blind.

Fast forward to **2025**, and the battleground looks different:

THEN (2000s)	NOW (2025)
Static malware	Polymorphic, AI-mutating malware
Fixed attack patterns	Adaptive, AI-generated attack strategies
Rule-based firewalls	Behavioral and AI-driven network defence
Signature-based AV	Predictive, AI-augmented EDR

Attackers today use AI to:

- Automatically generate polymorphic malware that **changes itself** every few hours.
- Launch **automated spear-phishing** attacks tailored specifically to each target.
- Conduct **real-time evasion**, adjusting malware behavior based on detection attempts.

This means:

Reactive cybersecurity is dead. Proactive, predictive, AI-driven cybersecurity is the future.

The threat landscape evolves **at machine speed**. Human defenders alone cannot keep up without AI augmentation.

Real Example: SolarWinds and Nation-State Supply Chain Attacks

The SolarWinds attack (detected in late 2020) showed how sophisticated supply chain attacks can compromise thousands of organizations silently. Attackers inserted malicious code into legitimate updates — bypassing traditional defences.

Had defenders relied **only on signature-based tools**, SolarWinds would have remained invisible for much longer. **Behavioral AI models** — detecting unusual network traffic, irregular login patterns, or minor anomalies — are now essential to spot such complex threats.

This is **our reality** in 2025 and beyond.

1.2 What Is Artificial Intelligence (AI) in Cybersecurity?

☐ AI Defined — Simply

At its core, **Artificial Intelligence (AI)** is:

Systems and algorithms that simulate human-like abilities: learning, adapting, deciding, predicting.

When applied to cybersecurity, AI can:

Detect anomalies
Recognize new patterns of attack
Predict vulnerabilities before they are exploited
Automate complex decision-making processes

Core AI Techniques Used in Cybersecurity

Technique	What It Means	Cybersecurity Application
Machine Learning (ML)	Algorithms that learn from data	Detect phishing, classify malware, predict threats
Deep Learning (DL)	Neural networks with many layers, modelling complex patterns	Recognize attack behaviors, natural language understanding for threat reports
Natural Language Processing (NLP)	Understanding and generating human language	Analyse threat intelligence reports, detect social engineering
Reinforcement Learning (RL)	Learning through trial and error and rewards	Optimize security automation decisions, adaptive defence
Generative AI (GANs, LLMs)	Models that create new content (text, images, malware)	Offensive AI (e.g., generating deepfakes), defensive summarization of incidents

Real Example: Microsoft's Security Copilot

In 2024, Microsoft released **Security Copilot** —
an AI security assistant using OpenAI's GPT models trained on Microsoft's threat data.

It helps analysts by:

- Summarizing incidents
- Recommending actions

- Automating incident investigation

It's the **beginning** of AI security co-pilots being **mainstream tools** inside every SOC (Security Operations Center).

1.3 Why AI Changes Everything in Cybersecurity

📈 Speed, Scale, and Sophistication

Speed:
AI can process billions of log entries, file behaviors, or network packets in minutes — a task impossible for human analysts.

Scale:
AI models can be trained on **terabytes of data**, spanning millions of endpoints and users.

Sophistication:
AI can **find hidden patterns** across multiple signals that are too subtle or complex for traditional rule-based systems.

It no longer matters **how many attacks** are launched.
It matters whether you can **recognize the hidden ones**.

Case Study: CrowdStrike's Falcon Platform

CrowdStrike uses **behavioral AI**:

- It collects endpoint telemetry (process starts, registry changes, file writes).

- Trains AI models to recognize "normal" behavior.

- Flags deviations even **if the malware is brand new** (no signature yet).

Result:
Falcon detects sophisticated ransomware (like Maze, Ryuk)

before traditional antivirus programs even generate signatures.

1.4 Understanding Machine Learning in Cybersecurity

Supervised Learning

In **supervised learning**, the model is trained on **labelled data** (e.g., "this file is malware", "this file is clean").

Example	Usage
Email marked as spam or not	Train spam filters
Executables labelled malware/benign	Malware detection models

Common Algorithms:

- Decision Trees
- Random Forests
- Support Vector Machines (SVM)
- Neural Networks

Unsupervised Learning

In **unsupervised learning**, the model finds **hidden patterns** without labelled data.

Example	Usage
Clustering login behaviors	Find insider threats
Grouping similar network traffic	Detect botnets

Common Algorithms:

- K-Means Clustering
- Isolation Forests (Anomaly Detection)
- Principal Component Analysis (PCA)

Deep Learning

Deep Learning involves **neural networks** with many hidden layers.
They can model highly complex, nonlinear relationships.

Example	Usage
CNNs (Convolutional Neural Networks)	Malware image classification
RNNs (Recurrent Neural Networks)	Detect sequence anomalies in API calls or system logs

Python Libraries for Machine Learning in Cybersecurity

Library	Purpose
scikit-learn	Traditional ML: decision trees, clustering, anomaly detection
TensorFlow / Keras	Build deep learning models
PyTorch	Advanced deep learning (preferred for research and experimentation)
Pandas and NumPy	Data manipulation and feature engineering
spaCy, nltk, transformers	NLP for cybersecurity text analysis

1.5 Python + AI + Cybersecurity = A Winning Formula

Python is the glue that connects:

- Raw security data
- Machine learning models
- Threat intelligence feeds
- APIs of modern security platforms

Python unlocks possibilities:

- Build your own anomaly detection engine
- Automate threat intelligence processing
- Create AI-driven malware classifiers
- Connect with cloud APIs to manage and secure infrastructure

And because of its huge community and mature libraries, **learning Python for cybersecurity AI is easier than ever**.

Example: Mini Python Snippet to Detect Anomalies (Introductory)

```python
from sklearn.ensemble import IsolationForest

import numpy as np


# Example network data: [duration, src_bytes, dst_bytes]

X = np.random.rand(100, 3)


# Train an Isolation Forest

clf = IsolationForest(random_state=42)
```

```
clf.fit(X)
```

```
# Predict anomalies
predictions = clf.predict(X)
```

```
# Find anomalies
anomalies = X[predictions == -1]
print("Anomalies detected:", anomalies)
```

Step-by-Step Explanation:

1. **Import libraries**: IsolationForest is a tree-based model that isolates anomalies.
2. **Generate dummy data**: Random network session data.
3. **Fit the model**: Learn "normal" behavior from the data.
4. **Predict**: Classify each session as normal (1) or anomaly (-1).
5. **Print anomalies**: View unusual network events!

Later in the book, we'll work with **real security data** (logs, flow records, file hashes).

1.6 The Challenges of Using AI in Cybersecurity

AI is powerful — but it's not a silver bullet.

There are challenges:

Challenge	Why It Matters
Data quality	Garbage in, garbage out. Bad data leads to bad models.
Adversarial attacks	Attackers can fool ML models with adversarial inputs.
Explainability	Deep models are often "black boxes"; hard to justify decisions.
Resource demands	Deep learning models can be heavy to train and deploy.
Continuous adaptation	Attackers evolve; models must retrain constantly.

Real Example: Adversarial Attacks on Malware Classifiers

Researchers have shown that carefully **modifying malware binaries** can cause ML classifiers to misclassify them as benign — without breaking the malware's function.

This shows:

Defenders must **harden AI models**.
Cyber-AI must be **robust, explainable, and adaptive**.

1.7 Strategic Mindset for AI Cybersecurity Professionals

You are not just learning technology.
You are learning strategy.

The best cybersecurity professionals:

- Think like **attackers** — to anticipate their moves.

- Think like **defenders** — to design strong protections.
- Think like **analysts** — to interpret data wisely.
- Think like **engineers** — to build and automate systems.
- Think like **leaders** — to drive innovation safely and ethically.

AI is just a tool.
Your mind is the real weapon.

This book will train you to use both.

Summary of Chapter 1

- Cybersecurity has evolved from static to dynamic AI-driven defence.
- AI helps defenders **scale detection, prediction, and prevention**.
- Python is the **language of AI cybersecurity**.
- Machine Learning, Deep Learning, and NLP are critical skills.
- AI enhances capabilities but requires careful, ethical, adaptive use.
- The future belongs to those who combine **technical skills with strategic thinking**.

Chapter 2: Offensive AI — When Hackers Turn Smart

2.1 Introduction: The Rise of AI-Powered Threat Actors

Artificial intelligence isn't just for defenders anymore. It's also becoming the most powerful weapon in the hands of attackers.

Since 2023, there has been a documented rise in **AI-enhanced cyberattacks**:

- **Phishing campaigns** that adapt their style dynamically based on the target's social media activity.
- **Deepfake voice scams** used to impersonate CEOs in real-time phone calls.
- **Adversarial malware** that **learns** which defences it faces and **alters itself** to evade detection.

AI allows threat actors to **scale**, **customize**, and **automate** attacks at levels previously impossible for human attackers alone.

 The **goal of this chapter** is to **understand these AI-enhanced offensive techniques** —
so you can **predict, defend, and counteract them.**

2.2 Offensive AI Techniques: Overview

Here's a structured overview of the major offensive AI techniques:

Technique	Attack Vector	Example
AI-Generated Phishing	Email, SMS, LinkedIn, WhatsApp	Personalized fake emails imitating your boss

Technique	Attack Vector	Example
Deepfake Attacks	Audio, Video	CEO voice scam calls
AI-Assisted Malware	Endpoint infections, ransomware	Malware that adapts its signatures dynamically
Adversarial Machine Learning	Attacks on ML models	Bypassing image or traffic-based AI detectors
Automated Vulnerability Scanning	Penetration testing and reconnaissance	AI that finds flaws faster than human pentesters

We will now **deep dive into each**, providing:

- **Real-world case studies**
- **Concept explanations**
- **Python-based demonstrations** where possible

2.3 AI-Generated Phishing and Social Engineering

How It Works

Phishing used to involve:

- Poorly worded emails
- Basic templates
- Broad "spray and pray" attacks

Today, with AI:

- Phishing emails are **customized** per target.

- Natural Language Generation models (GPT-4 class or fine-tuned LLMs) craft **perfect, human-like** messages.

- Attackers scrape **social media** for context (LinkedIn posts, Twitter bios) and train models to **mimic company language**.

Real-World Example: AI Phishing in the Wild

In 2024, security researchers at IBM X-Force Red demonstrated an AI-driven phishing engine.

- They trained a GPT-3.5 model on 100,000 corporate emails (non-sensitive, public communications).

- The AI then generated phishing emails that achieved a **click-through rate of 48% — triple** the success rate of traditional phishing kits.

Python Example: Simple Phishing Message Generator (Conceptual)

(For educational purposes only — strictly defensive understanding.)

```
import random


# Simple templates

openers = [

    "Hope you're doing well,",

    "Following up on our previous conversation,",

    "I urgently need your help with the project,"

]
```

```
requests = [
    "Can you send me the updated report?",
    "Please review the attached document.",
    "Kindly authorize the payment urgently."
]


signoffs = [
    "Best regards, John",
    "Thanks, CFO Office",
    "Appreciate your prompt response, Legal Team"
]


def generate_phishing_email():
    return f"{random.choice(openers)}
{random.choice(requests)} {random.choice(signoffs)}"


print(generate_phishing_email())
```

Step-by-Step Code Explanation:

- We define sets of opening lines, requests, and sign-offs.

- Randomly **assemble a coherent phishing email**.

- In real offensive AI, much **more complex models** (transformers) generate text conditioned on the target's context.

Strategic Insight: Red Teaming Defensive AI

Companies now **red-team** their own phishing simulations using AI.

- They pretrain LLMs on internal communication patterns.

- Test whether internal employees are vulnerable.

Lesson:
Defensive teams must **expect customized phishing** as a default — not the exception.

Best defence:

- Regular phishing simulations

- AI-assisted training

- Behavioral baselining (e.g., email from boss but unusual time/location triggers alert)

2.4 Deepfakes as a Cyberweapon

How It Works

Deepfakes use **Generative Adversarial Networks (GANs)** or **diffusion models** to:

- Synthesize fake audio, video, and even real-time deepfake calls.

In cybercrime:

- Attackers deepfake a CEO's voice calling the CFO.

- Deepfake Zoom meetings trick employees into fraudulent wire transfers.

Real-World Example: Deepfake Voice Fraud Case

In 2023, an energy company in the UAE was scammed out of **$35 million** after a criminal group deepfaked a CEO's voice to authorize transfers.

The attackers used **public video/audio material** of the CEO to **train a GAN-based voice cloning model**.

Python Concept: Understanding Voice Cloning Frameworks

Popular libraries involved:

- Coqui TTS — for text-to-speech cloning.
- Descript's Overdub — commercial clone training.
- Real-Time-Voice-Cloning — open-source voice synthesis.

(Installation and training require ethical use and large datasets; educational exploration only.)

Defence Strategy: Deepfake Detection Techniques

To defend against deepfakes:

Defence	Technique
Audio watermarking	Embed inaudible markers
Liveness detection	Ask spontaneous questions in video calls
Deepfake detection AI	Classifiers trained to spot generation artifacts

---

2.5 AI-Assisted Malware and Mutating Ransomware

How It Works

AI allows malware to:

- **Morph itself**: E.g., changing obfuscation every time it replicates.

- **Learn defences**: Detect when it's running inside a virtual machine and alter behavior.

- **Plan attacks dynamically**: Choosing infection strategies based on observed system defences.

Real-World Example: Emotet Evolution

Emotet malware evolved using modularity:

- Adapting payloads depending on whether antivirus software was detected.

- Using encryption layers randomized per infection.

Future malware will likely use **AI decision trees** or **neural planners** to evolve live on compromised hosts.

Python Snippet: Conceptual Adaptive Behavior (Simulation)

```python
import random

def detect_environment():
    environments = ['VM', 'Real Machine', 'Sandbox']
    return random.choice(environments)


def choose_action(env):
```

```
if env == 'VM':

    return "Sleep to evade"

elif env == 'Sandbox':

    return "Self-delete"

else:

    return "Execute Payload"


environment = detect_environment()

action = choose_action(environment)


print(f"Detected: {environment} --> Action: {action}")
```

Step-by-Step:

- Randomly simulate environment detection.
- AI-based malware would make decisions dynamically based on system characteristics.

Defenders need behavioral monitoring, not just static detection.

2.6 Adversarial Machine Learning: Attacking the Defenders' AI

How It Works

Adversarial ML attacks involve:

- Crafting **inputs** (images, network traffic, binaries) designed to **fool AI models** into wrong classifications.

Example: Fooling Image-Based Malware Classifiers

Security researchers have shown that by adding **small perturbations** to malware binaries converted into images, they could cause CNN-based malware detectors to misclassify them as benign.

Python Concept: Adversarial Example Generation (Simple)

Libraries:

- CleverHans
- Foolbox

Example approach (theoretical):

1. Take malware binary.
2. Convert to grayscale image.
3. Apply minimal pixel changes that shift the model's prediction.

(Complex, but critical to understand.)

Defence Strategy:

- Use **adversarial training**: expose models to adversarial examples during training.
- **Model explainability tools** (like SHAP) to monitor unexpected feature sensitivities.

2.7 AI-Based Automated Reconnaissance and Scanning

How AI Enhances Recon

Tools like:

- Shodan AI-enhanced queries
- AI-recon agents scanning for vulnerable APIs, exposed databases

make **early-stage attacks faster and deeper**.

An AI scanner:

- Identifies technology stacks from HTTP headers automatically.
- Prioritizes scanning based on historical exploit data.

Python has libraries like shodan, enabling recon automation.

```
import shodan

API_KEY = "Your_Shodan_API_Key"
api = shodan.Shodan(API_KEY)

query = "port:22 country:US"
result = api.search(query)

for service in result['matches']:
    print(service['ip_str'], service['port'])
```

Example Usage:

- Scan for exposed SSH servers in the US.

- Build automated attack surface mapping.

Chapter 2 Summary

Key Takeaway	Why It Matters
Attackers now automate with AI	Scaling attacks far beyond human capability
Phishing, deepfakes, mutating malware, adversarial ML	New threats demand new defensive strategies
Python empowers understanding and defence	Build defensive automation, model hardening, detection AI

You must **anticipate AI-augmented adversaries** and **use AI yourself to stay ahead**.

Chapter 3: Defensive AI — Strengthening Cyber Defences

3.1 Introduction: Why Defence Needs AI Now More Than Ever

The scale of cyberattacks in 2025–2030 **is beyond human capacity to handle manually**.

Every day:

- Millions of login attempts happen globally.

- Thousands of malware variants emerge.

- Billions of network flows occur inside enterprise networks.

Without AI:

Analysts drown in false positives.
Incidents slip through unnoticed.
Threat actors move faster than response teams.

With AI:

- Threats are detected **in real time**.

- Anomalies are **flagged instantly**.

- Responses can be **automated** before damage escalates.

Thus, **Defensive AI** is not optional — it is now a **fundamental part of every cybersecurity operation**.

3.2 Core Functions of Defensive AI Systems

Function	Description	Example
Detection	Find threats and anomalies faster than humans can	Spot suspicious logins
Classification	Categorize events: benign vs malicious	Classify emails as phishing
Prediction	Anticipate future attacks based on behavior patterns	Predict insider threats
Response	Act autonomously or semi-autonomously to contain threats	Isolate compromised endpoints

AI amplifies **every phase** of cyber defence — from **proactive monitoring** to **rapid incident containment**.

3.3 AI-Driven Anomaly Detection Systems

What Is Anomaly Detection?

Anomaly detection refers to **identifying events or patterns that do not conform to expected behavior**.

Examples:

- A user logs in from Tokyo at 9 AM and from New York 10 minutes later.
- A process starts encrypting thousands of files in a short time span.
- A server suddenly transmits gigabytes of data to an unfamiliar IP.

These anomalies often indicate **security incidents**.

Real-World Case Study: Darktrace's Enterprise Immune System

Darktrace's AI analyses:

- Network traffic
- DNS requests
- Authentication logs

It builds a **"self-learning model"** of what normal behavior looks like
and **flags deviations** — even if the attack is completely novel.

Python Example: Building a Simple Anomaly Detector

Let's simulate **anomaly detection on network sessions**:

```
import numpy as np

from sklearn.ensemble import IsolationForest


# Simulate network session data: [duration_sec, bytes_sent, bytes_received]

X_normal = np.random.normal(loc=[30, 5000, 5000], scale=[10, 2000, 2000], size=(1000, 3))

X_anomalies = np.array([[300, 50000, 60000], [2, 100000, 5]]) # Outliers


X = np.vstack((X_normal, X_anomalies))


# Train Isolation Forest

clf = IsolationForest(contamination=0.01, random_state=42)

clf.fit(X)


# Predict anomalies

labels = clf.predict(X)

outliers = np.where(labels == -1)[0]


print(f"Anomalies found at indices: {outliers}")
```

Step-by-Step Code Explanation:

- **Create normal data** (simulating regular network sessions).

- **Inject anomalies** (extremely high or low traffic).

- **Train Isolation Forest**: learns what is "normal."

- **Predict anomalies**: finds sessions that don't fit normal patterns.

This basic concept is **how real systems** detect compromised accounts, rogue devices, or data exfiltration attempts.

Strategic Tip:

In production, **feature engineering** becomes critical:

- Time of day

- User role

- Geographic location

- Device type

More intelligent features → Better anomaly detection accuracy.

3.4 Endpoint Detection and Response (EDR) with AI

What Is EDR?

Endpoint Detection and Response refers to:

- Monitoring endpoint (laptops, servers) activity.

- Detecting suspicious behavior.

- Enabling rapid investigation and containment.

Modern EDR solutions embed **machine learning models** to catch threats **without relying only on known signatures**.

Real-World Case Study: CrowdStrike Falcon's Behavioral AI

CrowdStrike's Falcon platform uses:

- **Event telemetry**: file access, process creation, network connections.

- **Cloud-based machine learning models** to classify threats.

- **Behavioral correlation** to detect complex attack sequences (e.g., living off the land attacks).

Their models detect ransomware **before** it starts encrypting — by spotting telltale precursors.

Python Example: Feature Extraction for EDR ML Models

Suppose you collect this endpoint telemetry:

Feature	Example
Process Name	powershell.exe
Parent Process	winword.exe
Command Line Args	"-nop -enc ..."
Network Connections Opened	5

We can **vectorize** this data for machine learning.

```
import pandas as pd
from sklearn.preprocessing import LabelEncoder


data = pd.DataFrame({
    'process_name': ['powershell.exe', 'explorer.exe', 'powershell.exe'],
```

```
    'parent_process': ['winword.exe', 'explorer.exe',
'outlook.exe'],

    'network_connections': [5, 0, 8]

})


# Encode categorical variables

le = LabelEncoder()

data['process_name_enc'] =
le.fit_transform(data['process_name'])

data['parent_process_enc'] =
le.fit_transform(data['parent_process'])


X = data[['process_name_enc', 'parent_process_enc',
'network_connections']]

print(X)
```

Step-by-Step:

- **Process telemetry**: Convert categorical data (process names) into numeric features.
- **Prepare dataset**: Ready for training ML classifiers (e.g., random forests).

This **feature engineering** step is **critical** before applying ML.

Strategic Tip:

Training effective EDR AI requires:

- Large volumes of endpoint telemetry.
- Correct labels (attack vs benign sessions).

- Continuous retraining to adapt to new attack techniques.

3.5 Threat Hunting Automation with AI

What Is Threat Hunting?

Threat hunting = proactively searching your environment for hidden attackers **before alerts fire**.

AI helps by:

- Prioritizing suspicious activity automatically.
- Suggesting leads based on past threat intelligence.
- Discovering **patterns humans would miss**.

Real-World Case Study: Microsoft Sentinel and Fusion AI

Microsoft's Azure Sentinel uses **Fusion AI** to:

- Correlate alerts across different data sources.
- Prioritize multi-stage attacks automatically.

It greatly reduces the **investigation time** for security analysts.

Python Concept: Automating Threat Hunt Queries

Example: Hunt for anomalous DNS traffic.

```
import pandas as pd


# Simulate DNS logs
dns_logs = pd.DataFrame({
```

```
    'hostname': ['update.microsoft.com', 'maliciousdomain.xyz',
'login.google.com'],

    'query_type': ['A', 'A', 'AAAA'],

    'bytes_transferred': [100, 50000, 200]

})


# Simple rule: flag very high bytes

suspicious_queries = dns_logs[dns_logs['bytes_transferred'] >
10000]


print(suspicious_queries)
```

Real hunting systems apply **anomaly detection + threat intelligence enrichment + cross-signal correlation**.

3.6 Building Defensible AI Models

Key Defensive AI Best Practices:

Practice	Purpose
Data Augmentation	Make models more robust against unseen attacks
Adversarial Training	Harden models against adversarial examples
Model Explainability	Understand why models predict threats

Practice	Purpose
Continuous Learning	Retrain regularly as new threats emerge

Example: Adversarial Training Concept

Train your malware classifier on:

- Legitimate samples.
- Malware samples.
- Slightly modified malware samples ("adversarial" examples).

Helps AI detect subtle evasion attempts!

3.7 Challenges and Limitations of Defensive AI

Challenge	Impact
False Positives	AI may flag benign behavior incorrectly
False Negatives	AI may miss cleverly disguised attacks
Model Drift	Environment changes → Model degrades over time
Bias in Training Data	Models learn human biases (e.g., ignoring rare attack types)

Mitigation:

- Continuous model evaluation
- Regular retraining

- Hybrid human-AI decision workflows

Chapter 3 Summary

Key Takeaway	Why It Matters
Defensive AI is mandatory in 2025+ cybersecurity	Defenders must scale to match automated attackers
Anomaly detection, EDR, threat hunting are AI-enabled	Defenders can find hidden threats faster
Python empowers building, evaluating, and improving AI models	Practical skills = strategic advantage

Mastering **Defensive AI strategies** means mastering the **future of cyber defence**.

Chapter 4: Threat Intelligence Automation — AI for Smarter Threat Feeds

---

4.1 Introduction: Why Threat Intelligence Needs AI

Threat intelligence (TI) is at the core of proactive cybersecurity.

Traditionally, threat intelligence involved:

- Manually reading security blogs.
- Parsing through endless CSVs of indicators (IPs, URLs, hashes).
- Reactively updating firewall rules.

In 2025 and beyond, this manual process is **impossible**:

- New Indicators of Compromise (IOCs) emerge **every few minutes**.
- Attack Tactics, Techniques, and Procedures (TTPs) evolve **in real time**.
- Threat data volumes are measured in **terabytes per day**.

AI is now essential for:

- Gathering
- Processing
- Enriching
- Prioritizing
- Acting on threat intelligence **automatically**.

**Modern threat intelligence isn't collected manually.
It's farmed, sorted, prioritized, enriched, and actioned by AI.**

4.2 The Threat Intelligence Automation Pipeline

Stage	Action	Tools & AI Techniques
1. Data Collection	Pull IOCs, reports, telemetry	APIs, Web Scraping, Log Parsing
2. Data Enrichment	Add contextual info	Whois Lookups, Passive DNS, GeoIP
3. Data Correlation	Link indicators to campaigns	Graph Analysis, Clustering, NLP
4. Data Prioritization	Score and rank threats	Risk Scoring Algorithms, ML Models
5. Actionable Intelligence	Feed into SIEMs, Firewalls, Playbooks	API Automation, SOAR Integration

Python empowers every single stage.

Real-World TI Sources

- AlienVault OTX (Open Threat Exchange)
- IBM X-Force Exchange
- Cisco Talos
- Recorded Future APIs
- VirusTotal Public/Private APIs
- AbuseIPDB
- Shodan

All of these offer **Python-accessible APIs**!

4.3 Automating Threat Data Collection

Python Example: Pulling IOCs from VirusTotal

```python
import requests

API_KEY = 'your_virustotal_api_key'
url = 'https://www.virustotal.com/api/v3/ip_addresses/8.8.8.8'

headers = {
    "x-apikey": API_KEY
}

response = requests.get(url, headers=headers)

data = response.json()
print(data['data']['attributes'])
```

Step-by-Step Code Explanation:

- **Authenticate** with VirusTotal API.
- **Request threat data** for IP address 8.8.8.8.
- **Parse JSON** to extract attributes (e.g., maliciousness scores, detection engines, categories).

Imagine automating this for thousands of IPs every hour!

Pro Tip:

Batch your queries using asynchronous Python (aiohttp) to scale collection massively.

4.4 Enriching Indicators with AI

Indicators alone are **weak** without **context**.

Good enrichment tells you:

- Where was the domain registered?
- Is the IP from a known hosting provider?
- Does the hash match known malware families?
- Is there associated threat actor attribution?

Real-World Case: Recorded Future's AI Context Engine

Recorded Future uses:

- NLP to extract threat context from millions of open web sources daily.
- Graph analysis to link IOCs to TTPs and threat groups.

Python Example: WHOIS Lookup and Enrichment

```
import whois

domain = "example.com"
whois_info = whois.whois(domain)

print(f"Registrar: {whois_info.registrar}")
```

```
print(f"Creation Date: {whois_info.creation_date}")
print(f"Name Servers: {whois_info.name_servers}")
```

Now imagine an AI model that flags:

- Recently created domains
- Obscure registrars
- Frequent ownership changes

as **high-risk indicators** automatically!

4.5 Natural Language Processing (NLP) for Threat Reports

Many threat intelligence reports are **free-text PDFs or blogs**.

Without NLP, humans must manually:

- Read
- Summarize
- Extract IOCs

NLP models **automate** this extraction.

Python Example: Named Entity Recognition (NER) on Threat Reports

```
import spacy


nlp = spacy.load("en_core_web_sm")
```

```
doc = nlp("Detected new phishing campaign targeting
Office365 users from IP 203.0.113.5.")


for ent in doc.ents:

    print(ent.text, ent.label_)
```

Output:

Office365 ORG

203.0.113.5 IP

- ORG = Organization
- IP = IP Address

Extract actionable indicators from free text —
automatically.

Real-World Example: ThreatQuotient NLP Enrichment

ThreatQuotient's platform uses NLP models to parse blogs, paste sites, reports, and convert **unstructured text into structured threat intelligence**.

4.6 Correlating Indicators with Graph-Based AI

Why Graph Analysis?

Threat campaigns often:

- Use the same infrastructure (IP clusters, DNS records).
- Reuse malware codebases.
- Follow observable patterns.

Graph algorithms find these **hidden links**.

Graph Concept	Application
Nodes	IPs, Domains, Hashes
Edges	Relationships (same server, same threat actor)
Community Detection	Grouping related IOCs together

Python Example: Building a Simple Threat Graph

```
import networkx as nx


G = nx.Graph()


G.add_edge("192.168.1.5", "badserver.com")
G.add_edge("badserver.com", "eicar_test_file")
G.add_edge("eicar_test_file", "APT29")


nx.draw(G, with_labels=True)
```

 See visual relationships between indicators!

Libraries like:

- NetworkX (graph creation)
- PyVis (graph visualization)
- igraph (large-scale graph mining)

are critical in real TI automation.

4.7 Prioritizing Threat Intelligence with Machine Learning

When you have:

- 500,000 suspicious IPs
- 200,000 domain alerts
- 50,000 malware hashes

Which ones matter most?

AI models **score** indicators:

- Based on reputation.
- Based on past maliciousness rates.
- Based on connectedness to active threat campaigns.

Python Concept: Risk Scoring

Simple idea:

```python
def calculate_risk_score(age_days, reputation_score, enrichment_count):
    return (100 - reputation_score) + (0.5 * enrichment_count) - (0.1 * age_days)


# Lower reputation, more enrichment → higher risk
print(calculate_risk_score(age_days=10, reputation_score=30, enrichment_count=5))
```

Professional platforms combine:

- ML classifiers

- Threat likelihood prediction models
- Analyst feedback loops

to constantly **improve prioritization**.

4.8 Feeding Automated TI into Defences

SOAR (Security Orchestration, Automation and Response)

AI-enriched TI feeds into:

- Firewalls (blocking bad IPs)
- SIEMs (triggering high-fidelity alerts)
- EDR platforms (blacklisting hashes)

Python-driven **SOAR playbooks** automate:

```
# Example: Auto-block IPs in firewall
malicious_ips = ["203.0.113.5", "198.51.100.10"]

for ip in malicious_ips:
    print(f"Blocking {ip} in firewall...")
    # Simulated API call: firewall_api.block_ip(ip)
```

Instant automated defences based on **live threat intelligence**.

4.9 Challenges and Limitations of TI Automation

Challenge	Impact
False positives	Over-blocking legitimate traffic
Data overload	Triage fatigue if automation is naive
Source reliability	Not all threat feeds are accurate
Correlation complexity	Some indicators have ambiguous links

Best Practice:
Use **multiple data sources, feedback loops, AI-based correlation**.

Automation must be intelligent, not blind.

Chapter 4 Summary

Key Takeaway	Why It Matters
Threat intelligence is too large for manual handling	Automation is mandatory
Python empowers full TI pipelines	From collection to enrichment to action
AI improves context, correlation, prioritization	Smarter, faster, better threat defences

Mastering **Threat Intelligence Automation** makes you a **proactive defender** — not just a reactive responder.

Chapter 5: Predicting the Unknown — AI for Zero-Day Attack Detection

5.1 Introduction: The Nightmare of Zero-Day Attacks

Zero-Day Vulnerability:
A flaw in software that is unknown to the vendor and exploited by attackers before a fix exists.

Zero-day attacks are the deadliest because nobody — not even the developers — knows the weakness exists.

Traditional cybersecurity defences:

- Firewall rules
- Signature-based detection
- Static threat intelligence feeds

ALL FAIL when facing a true zero-day.

Only **AI-based behavior modelling**, **prediction systems**, and **dynamic threat analysis** offer hope.

5.2 Why Zero-Day Defence Must Be Predictive, Not Reactive

Modern zero-day attacks exploit:

- Unpatched third-party libraries (e.g., Log4j vulnerability)
- Misconfigurations in cloud environments
- Unseen flaws in authentication systems

In 2025–2030, **zero-day hunting** has shifted focus:

- From **finding known indicators**
- To **predicting unknown weaknesses** based on **patterns**, **anomalies**, and **behavior shifts**

Defensive AI must predict:

- Which systems are likely to harbor zero-days
- Which behaviors suggest active exploitation
- Which anomalies indicate early-stage compromise

5.3 Core AI Techniques for Predicting Zero-Day Threats

Technique	Purpose	Example
Anomaly Detection	Spot behavior deviations	New C2 patterns, strange DNS
Vulnerability Prediction Models	Predict risk areas in codebases	Libraries with poor update history

Technique	Purpose	Example
Graph-based Attack Surface Mapping	Understand potential attack chains	Lateral movement detection
Behavioral Baselines	Profile normal user/app behavior	Detect anomalies before signature exists

Real-World Case: Darktrace's Antigena Autonomous Response

Darktrace's AI-powered Antigena module:

- Monitors enterprise behavior.

- Detects **never-before-seen** attacks by spotting deviations.

- Automatically **isolates compromised devices** before the threat is understood.

Lesson:
You **can't wait for signatures** anymore.
You must **detect the unknown** at the behavior level.

5.4 Building a Behavioral Anomaly Detection System

Python Example: Training an Isolation Forest to Spot Suspicious Activity

Suppose you monitor **login behavior**:

Feature	Meaning
Login Hour	What hour the login occurred
Country	Country of login
Device Type	Laptop, Mobile, Tablet

You want to **detect strange logins**.

```python
import pandas as pd
from sklearn.ensemble import IsolationForest
from sklearn.preprocessing import LabelEncoder

# Simulated data
data = pd.DataFrame({
    'login_hour': [8, 9, 10, 15, 16, 22, 23, 2],
    'country': ['US', 'US', 'US', 'US', 'US', 'RU', 'CN', 'BR'],
    'device': ['Laptop', 'Laptop', 'Laptop', 'Laptop', 'Laptop', 'Mobile', 'Mobile', 'Tablet']
})

# Encode categorical data
le_country = LabelEncoder()
le_device = LabelEncoder()

data['country_enc'] = le_country.fit_transform(data['country'])
data['device_enc'] = le_device.fit_transform(data['device'])
```

```
X = data[['login_hour', 'country_enc', 'device_enc']]

# Train Isolation Forest
clf = IsolationForest(contamination=0.25, random_state=42)
clf.fit(X)

# Predict anomalies
labels = clf.predict(X)
data['anomaly'] = labels

print(data)
```

Step-by-Step Code Explanation:

- **Create login dataset** (hour, country, device type).
- **Label encode** text fields into numeric.
- **Train Isolation Forest** to learn "normal" login behavior.
- **Predict anomalies** (label -1 = anomalous behavior).

Strategic Tip:

- Train your models on "known good" behavior — not attack data.
- Let the model flag deviations — even if they aren't obvious threats yet.

5.5 Predicting Vulnerabilities in Code Using AI

Besides behavioral monitoring,
AI can **analyse source code** to predict:

Risky functions
Potential vulnerabilities
Areas needing security review

Feature Extracted from Code	Risk Indication
Function Length	Long functions = more error-prone
Nested Loops/Branches	Complex logic = more security risks
Use of Dangerous APIs	(e.g., strcpy, gets in C)
Missing Error Handling	Potential exploitable behavior

Research Example: OpenAI Codex for Vulnerability Discovery

In 2024, researchers trained Codex (a GPT variant) to:

- **Analyse code snippets**
- **Predict likely vulnerabilities** (e.g., buffer overflow risks)

Python Concept: Static Code Metrics

```python
def count_lines_of_code(code_text):
    return len([line for line in code_text.split('\n') if line.strip()])
```

```
sample_code = """
def unsafe_copy(src):
    buffer = [0]*10
    for i in range(len(src)):
        buffer[i] = src[i]  # Potential buffer overflow
"""
```

```
print(f"Lines of code: {count_lines_of_code(sample_code)}")
```

Simple static analysis like this can help build **risk scoring models** automatically.

Advanced approaches involve:

- Abstract Syntax Trees (AST parsing)
- ML-based vulnerability prediction (e.g., graph neural networks)

5.6 Using Graph AI to Predict Attack Paths

Attackers don't exploit vulnerabilities randomly.
They follow **logical paths**:

- User → Privilege Escalation → Lateral Movement → Domain Admin

AI can **map environments into graphs** and predict:

- Likely paths an attacker would take.
- Weak points needing reinforcement.

Node Device/User/Service

Edge Communication/Trust/Access relationship

Python Concept: Building Simple Attack Path Graphs

```python
import networkx as nx

G = nx.Graph()

G.add_edge('Workstation1', 'Server1')
G.add_edge('Server1', 'DomainController')
G.add_edge('Workstation2', 'Server1')

# Find all paths from Workstation2 to DomainController
paths = list(nx.all_simple_paths(G, source='Workstation2', target='DomainController'))

print(paths)
```

Predict **how attackers could move laterally** — then defend critical nodes first!

5.7 Early Warning Systems Using AI

Some companies build **early warning systems** using:

- Machine learning
- Open-source threat feeds
- Social media monitoring
- Dark web scraping
- Honeypot telemetry

AI clusters new incidents and flags **likely zero-day campaigns** before wide exploitation.

Example Systems:

- Google Chronicle's VirusTotal Intelligence
- Recorded Future's Attack Surface Intelligence

Key Early Signals:

- Sudden spike in unknown binaries
- Rise in abnormal traffic targeting specific ports
- New dark web chatter about vulnerabilities

5.8 Challenges in Predicting Zero-Days with AI

Challenge	Impact
Noise in data	Many anomalies are benign
Unknown unknowns	Truly new attacks may evade early models
Adversarial noise	Attackers may poison behavior models

Challenge	Impact
Resource limitations	Graphs and anomaly models can be computationally expensive

Solutions:

- Multi-layered models (ensemble methods).
- Feedback loops (human-AI cooperation).
- Prioritized monitoring of high-risk assets.

Chapter 5 Summary

Key Takeaway	Why It Matters
Zero-days bypass traditional defences	Only behavior-based AI can spot them early
Predictive modelling is critical	Not waiting for indicators, acting on deviations
Python empowers practical early warning systems	Data gathering, anomaly detection, attack path mapping

Predicting zero-days means shifting from **passive defence** to **active hunting**
— and AI makes it possible.

Chapter 6: AI in Cloud Security — Protecting Infrastructure at Scale

6.1 Introduction: Why Cloud Security Needs AI

The move to cloud computing has revolutionized IT infrastructure:

- Amazon Web Services (AWS)
- Microsoft Azure
- Google Cloud Platform (GCP)

But it also created a radically expanded attack surface:

- Millions of containers
- Billions of API calls
- Petabytes of unstructured, live telemetry

Humans alone cannot secure cloud environments anymore.

Cloud security in 2025–2030 depends on artificial intelligence to monitor, detect, and respond across dynamic, global infrastructure.

Traditional Cloud Security	AI-Augmented Cloud Security
Static policies (IAM, firewall)	Behavioral baselining and anomaly detection
Manual audits	Continuous automated risk scoring
Rule-based alerts	Predictive threat detection with ML
Slow incident response	Autonomous remediation actions

AI makes cloud security:

- **Real-time**
- **Scalable**
- **Predictive**

6.2 Unique Security Challenges in the Cloud

Key cloud-specific security risks:

Risk	Explanation
Identity Misconfigurations	Over-permissive IAM roles, leaked keys
API Exploits	Vulnerable or exposed APIs
Container Security Issues	Escapes, unscanned images, misconfigured runtimes
Shadow IT	Unmanaged assets spun up without security oversight

Risk	Explanation
Rapid Scale Changes	New resources added hourly, configurations drift

Cloud threats are:

- **Fast** (attack and exploit happen within minutes)
- **Ephemeral** (short-lived containers, serverless functions)
- **API-driven** (no traditional perimeter)

Only **dynamic, intelligent, behavior-driven AI** can cope.

6.3 AI for Cloud Threat Detection: Behavioral Monitoring

Cloud providers like AWS, Azure, and GCP collect enormous logs:

- AWS CloudTrail (API activity)
- VPC Flow Logs (network telemetry)
- CloudWatch Metrics (operational telemetry)

AI systems analyse these logs for anomalies, such as:

- A user downloading terabytes of data unusually fast
- API keys being used from unexpected geographies
- A container behaving abnormally (e.g., port scanning internally)

Real-World Case Study: AWS GuardDuty

- GuardDuty uses **unsupervised machine learning models** trained on massive telemetry.

- In 2024, GuardDuty introduced **ML-driven EKS (Kubernetes) threat detection**:
    - Monitoring pod behavior
    - Spotting suspicious API usage
    - Detecting crypto mining inside clusters

Python Concept: Analysing CloudTrail Data

Let's simulate a simple **anomaly detection** model:

```python
import pandas as pd

from sklearn.ensemble import IsolationForest


# Simulate CloudTrail-like event data

events = pd.DataFrame({

    'eventName': ['ListBuckets', 'PutObject', 'PutObject',
'DeleteObject', 'PutObject', 'PutObject'],

    'bytesTransferred': [100, 500, 400, 100, 12000, 14000],

    'sourceIP': ['1.2.3.4', '1.2.3.4', '1.2.3.4', '1.2.3.4', '8.8.8.8',
'8.8.8.8']

})


# Simple feature engineering

events['event_encoded'] =
events['eventName'].astype('category').cat.codes
```

```
# Train Isolation Forest
clf = IsolationForest(contamination=0.2, random_state=42)
X = events[['event_encoded', 'bytesTransferred']]
clf.fit(X)

labels = clf.predict(X)
events['anomaly'] = labels

print(events)
```

Step-by-Step:

- Encode event names numerically.
- Train Isolation Forest to find anomalies.
- Label events as -1 (anomalous) or 1 (normal).

In real-world platforms like AWS Macie (for S3 data), this same concept is scaled to millions of transactions daily!

6.4 AI in Identity and Access Management (IAM) Hardening

Identity is the new perimeter.

In cloud security, most breaches happen because:

- **Excessive permissions** (IAM misconfigurations)
- **Compromised credentials**

How AI Helps:

AI Role	Purpose
Analyse IAM policies	Detect over-permissioned roles
Behavior profiling	Flag unusual cross-account access
Risk-based access control	Dynamically adjust permissions based on behavior

Real-World Case Study: Microsoft Defender for Cloud

Defender for Cloud uses ML to:

- Analyse service principal behavior.
- Flag unusual cross-tenant authentications.
- Detect risky app registrations dynamically.

Python Concept: IAM Policy Analyser (Basic Model)

```python
import json


# Example IAM policy
policy = {
    "Statement": [
        {"Effect": "Allow", "Action": "*", "Resource": "*"},
        {"Effect": "Allow", "Action": "s3:ListBucket", "Resource":
"*"}
    ]
}
```

```
# Simple risk scoring: wildcard permissions are high risk
risk_score = 0
for statement in policy['Statement']:
    if "*" in statement['Action']:
        risk_score += 50
    else:
        risk_score += 10


print(f"IAM Policy Risk Score: {risk_score}")
```

Better practice:

- Train models on historical IAM breaches.
- Predict risky policies dynamically.
- Suggest automatic policy hardening (least privilege).

6.5 Container and Serverless Security with AI

Containers (Docker, Kubernetes) and **serverless (Lambda, Functions-as-a-Service)** are key cloud-native paradigms.

Security risks:

- Insecure images
- Supply chain attacks
- Container breakouts

- Excessive Lambda permissions

How AI Helps:

AI Application	Example
Container Behavior Analysis	Detect unexpected open ports, lateral scans
Image Static Analysis	ML classification of vulnerable Docker images
Serverless Function Monitoring	Flag strange invocation patterns

---

Real-World Case: Sysdig Secure and AI Behavior Profiling

Sysdig uses ML to:

- Learn container baselines
- Detect anomalies (e.g., a database container suddenly executing shell scripts)

Python Concept: Monitoring Unexpected Ports in Containers

```
# Simulated port access logs

container_ports = [80, 443, 22, 3306, 8080, 50000]  # 50000 is suspicious


# Known good ports

safe_ports = {80, 443, 8080}
```

```
suspicious = [port for port in container_ports if port not in
safe_ports]
```

```
print(f"Suspicious Ports Detected: {suspicious}")
```

In real deployments, AI profiles "normal" port behavior and flags new/unusual ports instantly.

6.6 AI for Cloud Security Posture Management (CSPM)

CSPM automates:

- Misconfiguration detection
- Compliance enforcement
- Continuous security assessment

AI enhances CSPM by:

- Predicting which misconfigurations are **most likely** to be exploited.
- Prioritizing critical findings based on historical breach data.

Real-World Case: Prisma Cloud by Palo Alto Networks

- Uses ML to score risks.
- Recommends least-privilege policies.
- Tracks compliance drift with behavioral baselines.

Example Common Cloud Misconfigurations:

- Open S3 buckets
- Unrestricted inbound security group rules
- Default admin passwords left unchanged

AI-Enhanced CSPM =
Not just flagging issues → **Predicting breach likelihoods**.

6.7 Autonomous Remediation with AI

Next frontier:
Not just alerting — auto-fixing!

Examples:

- Auto-revoking excessive IAM privileges.
- Auto-closing public S3 buckets.
- Auto-killing compromised Lambda functions.

Case Study: Azure Auto-Remediation Policies

Azure uses policies like:

- If open RDP port (3389) detected → **Automatically close** unless whitelisted.
- ML prioritization ensures only true positives are auto-remediated.

Auto-remediation reduces **response time to seconds**, not hours.

6.8 Challenges of AI in Cloud Security

Challenge	Why It's Hard
Data explosion	Millions of events/hour from large cloud deployments
False positives	Bad models can flood teams with noise
Dynamic environments	Models must retrain as cloud assets change
Cloud-specific adversarial attacks	Attackers learn cloud AI detection patterns

Solutions:

- Continuous retraining
- Ensemble models (multiple AI techniques together)
- Tight human-AI feedback loops

Chapter 6 Summary

Key Takeaway	Why It Matters
Cloud attacks are dynamic, fast, API-driven	Only AI can monitor effectively
AI enables real-time, behavior-based detection	Beyond static rules and signatures

Key Takeaway	Why It Matters
Python empowers cloud AI systems	Log parsing, anomaly detection, remediation scripting

Mastering AI-driven cloud security is essential for defending **modern infrastructures**
— and Python skills are your launchpad.

Chapter 7: AI in IoT Security — Defending Billions of Devices

---

7.1 Introduction: The IoT Explosion — A New Cybersecurity Frontier

---

Internet of Things (IoT) has transformed the world:

- Smart homes

- Smart cities
- Industrial IoT (IIoT)
- Healthcare devices
- Connected cars

By **2025**, there are **more than 30 billion connected IoT devices** worldwide.

 Every sensor, every camera, every smart lock is a potential point of attack.

IoT brings convenience — but it also massively expands the threat surface.

Real-World Example: Mirai Botnet Attack

- In 2016, the **Mirai** malware turned millions of insecure IoT devices (cameras, routers) into a botnet.
- It launched a **record-breaking DDoS attack** on DNS provider Dyn, causing major websites (Twitter, Netflix) to go offline.

Mirai exploited:

- Default passwords
- Unpatched firmware
- Poor device visibility

In 2025+, Mirai-class attacks are just the beginning:

- AI-enhanced IoT botnets
- Smart home targeting
- Critical infrastructure manipulation (industrial IoT)

Defending IoT requires **AI-based, real-time, distributed security systems** — built to handle **scale and heterogeneity**.

7.2 Unique Challenges of Securing IoT

Challenge	Why It's Hard
Limited device resources	Many devices can't run complex security software
Diversity of devices	Different OSes, architectures, protocols
Lack of standardization	Inconsistent security features across vendors
Physical accessibility	Devices in the wild are easier to tamper with
Update issues	Many devices have poor or no update mechanisms

Traditional endpoint security fails in the IoT world.

AI-based anomaly detection, behavioral modelling, and autonomous response are key.

7.3 AI for Anomaly Detection in IoT Networks

IoT devices usually follow **predictable behavior patterns**:

- A smart thermostat reports temperature every 10 minutes.

- A surveillance camera uploads video at regular intervals.
- A water pump controller adjusts based on sensor input.

Any deviation from these patterns could indicate:

- Malware infection
- Device takeover
- Data exfiltration
- Botnet recruitment

Python Example: IoT Device Traffic Anomaly Detection

```
import numpy as np

from sklearn.ensemble import IsolationForest


# Simulate normal telemetry: [reporting interval seconds, data size KB]

X_normal = np.random.normal(loc=[600, 50], scale=[50, 10], size=(1000, 2))


# Inject anomalies: weird intervals or huge data exfiltration

X_anom = np.array([[100, 1000], [5000, 10]])


X = np.vstack((X_normal, X_anom))


# Train Isolation Forest

clf = IsolationForest(contamination=0.01, random_state=42)

clf.fit(X)
```

```
labels = clf.predict(X)
outliers = np.where(labels == -1)[0]


print(f"Anomalous telemetry samples: {outliers}")
```

Step-by-Step:

- Normal telemetry around **600s intervals, 50KB data**.
- Outliers (e.g., 1-second interval, 1000KB upload) flagged.
- **Behavior-based detection** — no prior knowledge of malware signatures required.

This principle underpins **real-world IoT anomaly detection platforms**.

7.4 Edge AI for Localized, Real-Time Security

Edge AI = running lightweight ML models directly on IoT devices or gateways.

Why?

- **Latency**: Decisions must be instant (e.g., industrial safety shutdowns).
- **Bandwidth**: Raw data uploads can flood networks.
- **Privacy**: Sensitive data should stay local.

Real-World Case: Nvidia's Jetson Nano AI Edge Devices

- Tiny devices with onboard AI acceleration.

- Used in smart cameras, factory sensors, autonomous drones.

- Can run lightweight deep learning models for security monitoring.

Python Concept: Tiny Anomaly Model for Edge Devices

```python
from sklearn.linear_model import LogisticRegression
import numpy as np


# Simulated feature set
X_train = np.random.rand(1000, 5)
y_train = np.random.choice([0, 1], size=1000)  # 0=normal, 1=anomaly


# Very lightweight classifier
model = LogisticRegression()
model.fit(X_train, y_train)


# Prediction
sample = np.random.rand(1, 5)
print(f"Prediction: {model.predict(sample)}")
```

Such simple models can be optimized to run **on microcontrollers or lightweight edge nodes**.

7.5 AI for IoT Device Authentication and Trust

Problem:
Spoofed IoT devices could connect to networks, impersonating legitimate devices.

Solution:
Device fingerprinting + AI classification.

Fingerprint Features	Examples
Packet timings	Transmission intervals
Power usage patterns	Current draw signatures
Wireless signal characteristics	RSSI, WiFi signal fluctuations
Device behavior profiles	Normal network interaction patterns

Train AI models to:

- Profile normal device signatures.
- Detect fake/spoofed devices immediately.

Real-World Example: Google's Brillo OS Fingerprinting

- Google researchers developed fingerprinting techniques for IoT devices.
- ML models detect anomalies based on **transmission patterns** even without accessing device firmware.

Python Concept: Simple Device Behavior Classifier

```python
from sklearn.tree import DecisionTreeClassifier


# Simulate device fingerprint features: [avg packet interval, avg packet size]
X = np.array([
    [5.0, 50], [5.2, 52], [4.9, 49],  # Legitimate device
    [10.0, 150], [9.8, 140], [11.2, 160]  # Spoofed device
])


y = np.array([0, 0, 0, 1, 1, 1])  # 0=legit, 1=spoofed


clf = DecisionTreeClassifier()
clf.fit(X, y)


# New device
sample = np.array([[5.1, 51]])
print(f"Device classified as: {clf.predict(sample)} (0=legit, 1=spoofed)")
```

Python enables building **basic device authentication models** that can be expanded for full network-scale IoT security.

7.6 Predictive Maintenance with AI for Industrial IoT (IIoT)

In industrial settings:

- Pumps, turbines, compressors are connected.
- Breakdowns = huge losses.

AI can:

- Monitor sensor data (vibration, temperature, voltage).
- Predict equipment failure **before** it happens.
- Trigger preventive actions (shutting down, repairs).

Real-World Case: Siemens MindSphere IoT Platform

- Collects IIoT telemetry.
- Uses deep learning models to detect abnormal machine behavior early.

Python Example: Simple Predictive Maintenance Model

```
from sklearn.ensemble import RandomForestClassifier

import numpy as np


# Simulate machine sensor data: [vibration, temperature, voltage]

X = np.random.rand(1000, 3)

y = np.random.choice([0, 1], size=1000)  # 0=healthy, 1=failure soon


clf = RandomForestClassifier()

clf.fit(X, y)
```

```
# New machine reading
sample = np.random.rand(1, 3)
print(f"Failure risk prediction: {clf.predict(sample)}")
```

Predictive maintenance saves millions by **fixing problems before catastrophic failures**.

7.7 Challenges in AI-Driven IoT Security

Challenge	Impact
Limited compute resources	Edge devices can't run heavy models
Heterogeneous data	Different devices produce different telemetry formats
Privacy concerns	Data collection must respect regulations (GDPR, HIPAA)
Concept drift	Device behavior changes over time, retraining needed
Physical attacks	AI can't stop hardware tampering alone

Solutions:
- Optimize models for edge deployment (TensorFlow Lite, ONNX).
- Standardize data collection formats.
- Implement privacy-preserving machine learning (federated learning).

- Regular model retraining and anomaly model updating.

Chapter 7 Summary

Key Takeaway	Why It Matters
IoT greatly expands the attack surface	AI is needed to monitor billions of endpoints
Behavioral anomaly detection is key	Signature-based security fails for diverse devices
Edge AI enables local real-time decision making	Scalability and privacy demands
Python empowers practical AI models for IoT	From anomaly detection to predictive maintenance

IoT Security is the next massive cybersecurity battleground —

and mastering **AI-based defences** will be essential to defend the physical world itself.

Chapter 8: AI in Blockchain and Smart Contract Security

8.1 Introduction: Blockchain — Revolutionary but Vulnerable

Blockchain has disrupted:

- Finance (cryptocurrencies like Bitcoin, Ethereum)
- Digital identity
- Supply chain management
- Smart contracts and decentralized applications (dApps)

It brings promises:

- **Decentralization**
- **Transparency**
- **Immutability**

However, blockchain systems are **not inherently secure**:

- Code bugs
- Smart contract vulnerabilities
- Fraudulent transactions
- Insider threats

Smart contracts are immutable — but their vulnerabilities are too. Once deployed, you cannot easily patch mistakes.

Real-World Example: The DAO Hack (Ethereum, 2016)

- Vulnerability in a smart contract.
- $60 million worth of ETH was stolen.

- Ethereum community had to fork the blockchain to recover.

Lesson:

Bugs in blockchain systems are catastrophic and **must be prevented proactively**.

AI can help detect flaws, predict fraud, and monitor blockchain behavior dynamically.

8.2 Core Blockchain and Smart Contract Threats

Threat Type	Example
Smart Contract Vulnerabilities	Reentrancy bugs, integer overflows
Transaction Fraud	Double spending, flash loan attacks
Node Compromise	Malicious miners, validator misbehavior
Privacy Leakage	De-anonymizing blockchain addresses
Consensus Attacks	51% attacks, selfish mining

Traditional security tools are ineffective on blockchain because:

- Transactions are public.
- Contracts are immutable.
- Attack patterns are **behavioral**, not signature-based.

AI excels at behavioral analysis, anomaly detection, and static code analysis — **critical for blockchain security.**

8.3 AI for Smart Contract Vulnerability Detection

How AI Helps:

- Analyse smart contract source code.
- Detect risky coding patterns.
- Predict possible exploits.

Technique	Application
Static code analysis	Parse contract code and find patterns
AST (Abstract Syntax Tree) parsing	Understand contract structure programmatically
ML classifiers	Predict whether a function is vulnerable
Deep learning	Discover complex code anomalies

Real-World Case Study: SmartCheck

- Static analyser for Solidity smart contracts.
- Finds common bugs (reentrancy, timestamp dependency, unprotected functions).
- AI-enhanced models are improving detection accuracy.

Python Concept: Simple Smart Contract Analyser (AST Example)

```python
import ast


# Example Solidity-like function (Python-style for simulation)
code = """
def withdraw(amount):
    if balance >= amount:
        send(amount)
    balance -= amount
"""


tree = ast.parse(code)


for node in ast.walk(tree):
    if isinstance(node, ast.FunctionDef):
        print(f"Function: {node.name}")
    if isinstance(node, ast.Call) and isinstance(node.func, ast.Name) and node.func.id == 'send':
        print(f"Send function found: possible reentrancy risk")
```

Step-by-Step Explanation:

- Parse code into an Abstract Syntax Tree (AST).
- Find sensitive functions (send, transfer in Solidity).
- Flag them for manual or automated deeper analysis.

Basic idea behind static analysers like **Mythril** or **Slither**.

8.4 AI for Blockchain Transaction Fraud Detection

Blockchain transactions are:

- **Permanent**
- **Pseudonymous**
- **Globally visible**

Attackers exploit:

- Flash loans
- Oracle manipulation
- Front-running attacks

How AI Helps:

AI Technique	Use Case
Transaction clustering	Group similar malicious transactions
Anomaly detection	Spot unexpected transfer behaviors
Graph analysis	Link suspicious wallets and transactions
Predictive modelling	Flag likely fraudulent behaviors early

Real-World Example: Chainalysis and AI in Crypto AML

- Uses machine learning to:
  - Cluster wallets

- Predict illegal transactions (money laundering, darknet markets)
- Map criminal blockchain networks

Python Example: Simple Blockchain Transaction Anomaly Detection

```python
import numpy as np

from sklearn.ensemble import IsolationForest


# Simulate transaction data: [transfer_amount, transaction_frequency]

X = np.random.normal(loc=[1000, 5], scale=[300, 2], size=(1000, 2))


# Add anomalous large transfer

X = np.vstack((X, [[100000, 1], [90000, 1]]))


# Train Isolation Forest

clf = IsolationForest(contamination=0.01, random_state=42)

clf.fit(X)


labels = clf.predict(X)

outliers = np.where(labels == -1)[0]


print(f"Suspicious transactions at indices: {outliers}")
```

How this works:

- Normal transactions have moderate values/frequency.
- Outliers (huge amounts, low frequency) are flagged.
- Extendable to multi-featured blockchain data.

8.5 Graph-Based Fraud Analysis on Blockchain

Blockchain can be visualized as a **transaction graph**:

- **Nodes** = Wallets/Addresses
- **Edges** = Transactions (flows of crypto)

AI can detect fraud rings, laundering cycles, and hidden relationships.

Graph AI Technique	Application
Community Detection	Find tightly-connected wallets
Centrality Analysis	Identify influential accounts
Link Prediction	Predict new suspicious connections forming

Python Concept: Wallet Transaction Graph

```
import networkx as nx


G = nx.DiGraph()
```

```
# Sample transactions: (sender, receiver, amount)
transactions = [('A', 'B', 10), ('B', 'C', 20), ('C', 'A', 5), ('A', 'D', 100000)]


for sender, receiver, amount in transactions:
    G.add_edge(sender, receiver, weight=amount)


# Find high-weight suspicious edges
for u, v, data in G.edges(data=True):
    if data['weight'] > 50000:
        print(f"Suspicious transaction: {u} -> {v} : {data['weight']} coins")
```

Real systems scale this to **millions of addresses**, using AI to cluster and rank threats.

8.6 AI for Smart Contract Behavior Monitoring

Even if smart contracts are secure at deployment, their **runtime behavior** can become suspicious.

AI can:

- Monitor function call sequences.
- Detect deviations from normal usage patterns.
- Spot sudden abnormal usage spikes.

Application	Example
Behavioral anomaly detection	Flashloan attack detection
Usage prediction	Model contract invocation frequency patterns
Access control monitoring	Spotting unauthorized function calls

Real-World Example: OpenZeppelin Defender

- Monitors deployed smart contracts.
- Uses machine learning to alert on unusual activity (abnormal token minting, governance proposal flooding).

8.7 Predictive Risk Scoring for Smart Contracts

Before users interact with dApps, they want to know:

- Is this contract safe?
- Has it been exploited before?
- How risky is it compared to others?

AI models **score contracts** based on:

- Code features
- Deployment metadata
- External behavioral metrics

Outputs:

- Trust scores
- Exploit likelihood predictions
- User-friendly risk labels

8.8 Challenges of Applying AI in Blockchain Security

Challenge	Why It's Hard
Noisy, sparse data	Especially for new contracts and transactions
Adversarial evasion	Attackers modify behavior to bypass AI detection
Label scarcity	Few labelled fraud examples available for supervised training
Interpretability	Black-box ML models are harder to audit legally
Scale	Full blockchain analysis = massive computation needed

Solutions:

- Combine multiple AI techniques (ensemble learning).
- Use semi-supervised and unsupervised models.
- Build explainable AI outputs (SHAP, LIME interpretations).

Chapter 8 Summary

Key Takeaway	Why It Matters
Blockchain is revolutionary but not invincible	Vulnerabilities and fraud exist at multiple layers
Smart contracts need proactive AI auditing	Prevent expensive, irreversible exploits
Behavioral and graph-based AI detects blockchain threats	Beyond static code analysis
Python empowers blockchain AI tools	Smart contract analysis, transaction monitoring, fraud detection

In the blockchain world, **trust is programmatic — and so is risk.**
AI is the only way to monitor, predict, and protect decentralized systems at scale.

Chapter 9: Essential Tools, Platforms, and Frameworks for AI Cybersecurity

9.1 Introduction: Why Tools and Frameworks Matter

Mastery of AI cybersecurity is not just about **concepts** — it's also about knowing how to **practically build, deploy, and manage systems**.

The right tools and frameworks turn theory into action.

Without them:

- Data stays raw.
- Models stay untrained.
- Anomalies stay hidden.
- Threats stay undetected.

In 2025–2030, cybersecurity professionals must command a powerful arsenal of open-source and commercial tools.

This chapter gives you a **full hands-on map**.

9.2 Essential Python Libraries for AI Cybersecurity

Library	Purpose
scikit-learn	Classic machine learning (classification, regression, clustering)
TensorFlow/Keras	Deep learning (neural networks, CNNs, RNNs)
PyTorch	Flexible, dynamic deep learning
XGBoost/LightGBM	Gradient boosting models (very powerful for structured security data)
Pandas	Data manipulation, cleaning, exploration

Library	Purpose
NumPy	Numeric operations, tensor processing
Matplotlib/Seaborn	Visualization of results, anomalies
spaCy/nltk/transformers	Natural Language Processing (NLP) for threat report analysis

Example: Using scikit-learn for Quick Model Building

```
from sklearn.ensemble import RandomForestClassifier

from sklearn.datasets import make_classification


# Simulated security dataset

X, y = make_classification(n_samples=1000, n_features=20, n_classes=2, random_state=42)


model = RandomForestClassifier()

model.fit(X, y)


print(f"Model accuracy: {model.score(X, y)}")
```

Build simple classifiers quickly, scale up to complex detection systems later.

9.3 AI Cybersecurity Frameworks and Platforms

Beyond libraries, full platforms integrate:

- Data ingestion

- Feature extraction

- Model training

- Deployment

- Monitoring

These platforms speed up building real-world defensive systems.

Platform	Purpose	Example Use Case
Apache Kafka	Real-time data streaming	SIEM event pipeline
Elastic Stack (ELK)	Log aggregation, search, dashboarding	Anomaly monitoring
Splunk with MLTK (Machine Learning Toolkit)	SIEM + ML integration	Predictive alerting
AWS SageMaker	Cloud machine learning workflows	SOC ML model hosting
Azure Sentinel	Cloud-native SIEM + SOAR	Threat detection and response
TensorFlow Extended (TFX)	ML pipeline management	End-to-end deployment of cyber-AI models

9.4 Threat Intelligence Automation Tools

You can't build threat intelligence pipelines manually.

These tools allow Python integration:

Tool	Purpose
MISP (Malware Information Sharing Platform)	IOC sharing and collaboration
OpenCTI	Threat actor knowledge graph
VirusTotal API	File, URL, IP reputation enrichment
Shodan API	Device exposure and vulnerability scanning

Example: Querying Shodan for Exposed Devices

```
import shodan

api = shodan.Shodan('Your_API_Key')

results = api.search('default password')

for result in results['matches']:
    print(result['ip_str'], result['org'], result['data'])
```

Find misconfigured devices worldwide (for defensive purposes!).

9.5 Specialized Open Source Security AI Projects

In 2025, open-source AI security projects are thriving.

Some must-know names:

Project	Description
DeepExploit	Automated penetration testing using reinforcement learning
Snort + ML Extensions	AI-enhanced intrusion detection system
Suricata + Zeek + AI pipelines	High-speed network threat detection with ML
MITRE ATT&CK + Machine Learning	Threat behavior modelling datasets

Real-World Example: DeepExploit

- Uses reinforcement learning (RL) to automatically plan and execute penetration tests.

- Python-based.

- Extensible to customize against different network environments.

9.6 Important Security Data Sources for AI Training

No data = no machine learning.

These sources provide **real-world datasets** for training, testing, and improving models:

Source	Dataset Type
CICIDS (Canadian Institute for Cybersecurity)	Real-world intrusion detection datasets
UNSW-NB15	Network packet captures with attacks
MIT Lincoln Lab DARPA 1998/1999	Classic cyber attack datasets
Kaggle Cybersecurity Challenges	Various cybersecurity competitions and datasets
VirusShare	Malware samples (be cautious, legal restrictions)

Pro Tip:

- Always split data into **training** and **testing** sets.
- Be careful with **class imbalance** (attacks are often rare events in real data!).

9.7 Frameworks for Adversarial Machine Learning Defence

Adversarial ML = when attackers try to trick your AI models.

Defensive frameworks:

Framework	Purpose
CleverHans	Adversarial attack generation (test your models)

Framework	Purpose
IBM Adversarial Robustness Toolbox (ART)	Build defences against adversarial inputs
Foolbox	Model testing against evasion attacks

Example: Simple Adversarial Example with CleverHans

```
from cleverhans.tf2.attacks import fast_gradient_method

import tensorflow as tf


model = tf.keras.models.load_model('your_model.h5')


# Simulated input

x = tf.random.normal((1, 28, 28, 1))


# Create adversarial example

x_adv = fast_gradient_method(model, x, eps=0.1, norm=np.inf)


prediction = model(x_adv)

print(prediction)
```

Test model robustness against evasion attempts.

9.8 Platforms for Security Data Visualization and Alerting

Making sense of AI outputs visually = critical for operational success.

Best options:

Platform	Description
Kibana	Visualize Elasticsearch data (logs, anomalies)
Grafana	Monitor ML metrics and security event KPIs
Splunk Dashboards	Create security alert visualizations
Power BI / Tableau	Business-level reporting of cybersecurity AI insights

---

Example: Basic Matplotlib Alert Visual

```
import matplotlib.pyplot as plt


# Simulated alert counts
alerts = ['Normal', 'Malware', 'Phishing', 'DDoS']
counts = [800, 50, 30, 20]


plt.bar(alerts, counts)
plt.title('Security Alerts This Week')
plt.show()
```

Even simple charts can **quickly convey operational risk levels**!

9.9 Important Commercial AI Cybersecurity Solutions to Know

Knowing commercial leaders helps you benchmark your own builds:

Vendor	Product
Darktrace	Enterprise AI Threat Detection
CrowdStrike Falcon	Behavioral AI for endpoints
SentinelOne Singularity	Autonomous endpoint protection
Vectra AI	AI for threat detection across cloud, data center, IoT
Palo Alto Cortex XDR	Integrated AI-driven detection and response

Many of these products:

- Integrate Python SDKs for custom workflows.
- Provide APIs for SOAR and SIEM integrations.
- Build upon **graph analysis**, **deep learning**, **automated behavior modelling**.

9.10 Strategy for Choosing the Right Tools

Best practices:

Principle	Application
Open-source when possible	Flexibility, customization
Platform-agnostic tools	Support multi-cloud, hybrid deployments
Modular architecture	Combine best-in-breed solutions
Focus on automation	Manual pipelines won't scale
Integrate explainability	Trace why AI makes specific decisions

Chapter 9 Summary

Key Takeaway	Why It Matters
Mastering tools turns knowledge into power	Hands-on ability to build real defences
Python is central to almost every platform	Automation, analysis, integration
AI cybersecurity tooling is expanding fast	Continuous learning of tools is mandatory

The **right tools + the right strategy**
= **unstoppable AI cybersecurity capability** for 2025 and beyond.

Chapter 10: Building Your First AI Cybersecurity System with Python: A Complete Project Walkthrough

10.1 Introduction: Why Build a Full System?

Until now, we've learned about:

- **AI techniques** (anomaly detection, prediction, behavioral profiling)
- **Python tools and frameworks**
- **Real-world threats and how AI addresses them**

Now, it's time to **build a full, working AI cybersecurity system —**
from raw data ingestion to actionable threat detection.

Theory without hands-on experience is hollow.
You're about to become a real AI cybersecurity practitioner.

10.2 Project Concept: Threat Anomaly Detection System (TADS)

Objective:
Build a Python-based system that:

- Collects simulated security telemetry (login attempts).
- Trains an AI model to detect anomalies.
- Flags suspicious behavior automatically.
- Outputs results for analyst review.

This mirrors real-world workflows in Security Operations Centers (SOCs).

Key Features of TADS:

Feature	Description
Data ingestion	Collect login events
Feature engineering	Transform raw data into ML-ready format
Model training	Build and validate anomaly detection models
Real-time scoring	Detect anomalies on new data
Result visualization	Help security analysts triage

10.3 Step 1: Setting Up the Project Environment

Required Libraries:

pip install pandas numpy scikit-learn matplotlib

Folder Structure:

tads_project/

    data/

    models/

    outputs/

    scripts/

Create separate folders for:

- Raw data (data/)
- Trained models (models/)
- Alert outputs (outputs/)
- Python scripts (scripts/)

10.4 Step 2: Simulating Security Event Data

We simulate login attempts:

Feature	Description
Username	User identifier
Source IP	Login origin
Timestamp	Time of login
Success/Failure	Login result
Attempt Duration	Time taken to attempt login (seconds)

Good logins: short duration, expected locations, daytime hours.
Suspicious logins: long attempts, strange IPs, odd times.

Python Script: Data Generation (scripts/generate_data.py)

```python
import pandas as pd
import numpy as np
from faker import Faker
import random


fake = Faker()


def generate_logins(n=1000):
    data = []
    for _ in range(n):
        username = fake.user_name()
        source_ip = fake.ipv4()
        timestamp = fake.date_time_this_year()
        success = random.choice([True, False, True, True])  # 75% successful
        duration = np.random.normal(loc=5, scale=2) if success else np.random.normal(loc=20, scale=10)
        duration = max(duration, 0.5)  # No negative durations
        data.append([username, source_ip, timestamp, success, duration])

    df = pd.DataFrame(data, columns=['username', 'source_ip', 'timestamp', 'success', 'attempt_duration_sec'])
    return df
```

```
# Save
df = generate_logins(5000)
df.to_csv('../data/login_events.csv', index=False)
```
Now we have 5,000 login records!

10.5 Step 3: Feature Engineering

Transform raw login events into AI-usable features:

Raw Feature Transformed Feature

Timestamp	Hour of day
IP address	Geolocation risk score (future improvement)
Username	Encode or generalize
Success	Boolean
Duration	Keep numeric

Python Script: Feature Preparation (scripts/prepare_features.py)

```python
import pandas as pd


df = pd.read_csv('../data/login_events.csv')


# Extract hour of login
df['hour'] = pd.to_datetime(df['timestamp']).dt.hour
```

```
# Encode success

df['success_encoded'] = df['success'].astype(int)


# Select features

features = df[['hour', 'success_encoded',
'attempt_duration_sec']]


features.to_csv('../data/features.csv', index=False)
```
Features ready for model training.

10.6 Step 4: Training the Anomaly Detection Model

We'll use an **Isolation Forest** — great for:

- Detecting outliers
- Unsupervised learning (no labels needed!)

Python Script: Model Training (scripts/train_model.py)

```
import pandas as pd

from sklearn.ensemble import IsolationForest

import joblib


# Load features

X = pd.read_csv('../data/features.csv')
```

```
# Train Isolation Forest
clf = IsolationForest(contamination=0.02, random_state=42)
clf.fit(X)


# Save model
joblib.dump(clf, '../models/tads_isolationforest.pkl')


print("Model trained and saved.")
```

 2% contamination assumes roughly 2% of logins are anomalous.

10.7 Step 5: Real-Time Detection (Simulated)

New login events arrive — we must detect anomalies!

Python Script: Anomaly Scoring (scripts/detect_anomalies.py)

```
import pandas as pd
import joblib


# Load model
clf = joblib.load('../models/tads_isolationforest.pkl')


# Load new batch of events
df = pd.read_csv('../data/features.csv')
```

```
# Predict
predictions = clf.predict(df)


# Anomaly: -1, Normal: 1
df['anomaly'] = predictions


# Save anomalies
anomalies = df[df['anomaly'] == -1]
anomalies.to_csv('../outputs/anomalies_detected.csv',
index=False)


print(f"{len(anomalies)} anomalies detected.")
```

 Detected suspicious logins!

10.8 Step 6: Visualization for Analysts

Plot alert distribution:

**Python Script: Visual Alerting
(scripts/visualize_alerts.py)**

```
import pandas as pd
import matplotlib.pyplot as plt


df = pd.read_csv('../outputs/anomalies_detected.csv')
```

```
plt.scatter(df['hour'], df['attempt_duration_sec'], c='red')

plt.title('Anomalous Login Events')

plt.xlabel('Hour of Day')

plt.ylabel('Attempt Duration (sec)')

plt.grid(True)

plt.show()
```

Instant visual:
Analysts see strange logins happening at odd hours with long durations.

10.9 Optional Enhancements

Possible project expansions:

- IP geolocation risk scoring (via external APIs)
- Alerting system (send Slack notifications)
- Model retraining pipeline (continuous learning)
- Multi-feature behavioral clustering
- Integrate with SIEM/SOAR tools (e.g., Elastic, Splunk)

10.10 Challenges and Lessons from Building a Full System

Challenge	Realization
Data Preprocessing	Raw data is messy. Feature engineering is key.

Challenge	Realization
Model Selection	No single best model — always experiment.
Evaluation	Manual review of flagged events critical (semi-supervised learning).
Scalability	System must be designed to grow (streaming pipelines, batch inference).
Feedback Loops	Analyst feedback should feed into future model improvements.

Chapter 10 Summary

Key Takeaway	Why It Matters
Full-stack knowledge matters	From data to model to detection
AI + Python is a powerhouse combo	End-to-end system with minimal code
Real-world security systems require pipelines	Not just isolated scripts
Visualization helps bridge tech and humans	Analysts need clarity, not raw data

You now **have the skills to build operational, real-world AI cybersecurity systems** — and this is just the beginning.

Chapter 11: The Future of AI in Cybersecurity 2030+

11.1 Introduction: Why Look Beyond 2030?

By 2030, artificial intelligence will not merely **assist** cybersecurity —
it will be **the core fabric of cyber defence and offense**.

The **speed, complexity, and autonomy** of cyber operations will increase exponentially.

This chapter is a **futures roadmap**:

- Anticipate where AI and cybersecurity are heading.
- Strategically prepare your skills, tools, and mindsets.

"If you see the future clearly, you own it."

11.2 Megatrends Shaping Cybersecurity and AI

Trend 1: Autonomous Cyber Defence

By 2030:

- Autonomous defence agents will continuously patrol cloud environments.
- Machine-on-machine cyber battles will occur without human initiation.

SOCs will have "AI first responders" executing:

- Instant containment
- Automated deception
- Self-healing systems

Trend 2: AI-Augmented Offense

Attackers will:

- Build autonomous malware that learns inside environments.
- Deploy fully AI-generated phishing and social engineering campaigns.
- Use reinforcement learning to find zero-days dynamically.

Offensive AI will be cheap, fast, and devastating — and defenders must use **stronger AI** to match.

Trend 3: Integration of AI in Critical Infrastructure

From hospitals to airports to financial systems:

- AI cybersecurity will protect **life-critical systems**.
- Attacks could endanger lives, not just data.

Cyberdefence becomes a **national security** and **public safety** priority.

Trend 4: Quantum Threats to Cryptography

By 2035–2040:

- Quantum computers could break traditional cryptographic schemes.

- Blockchain security, VPNs, TLS, and data encryption standards must evolve.

Post-quantum cryptography + AI-based key management will be necessary.

Trend 5: Ethical and Governance Challenges

AI systems will:

- Make high-stakes cybersecurity decisions autonomously.
- Force governments and companies to confront accountability issues.

Ethical AI in cybersecurity becomes **mandatory**, not optional.

11.3 Deep Dive: Autonomous SOCs (Security Operation Centers)

By 2030:

Aspect	Traditional SOC	Autonomous SOC
Alert triage	Manual by analysts	AI triages 99% automatically
Threat hunting	Human-driven	AI suggests hunt targets
Response	Playbooks by humans	Dynamic, AI-generated response actions
Learning	Manual rule updates	Continuous self-learning AI

Human analysts become:

- Supervisors
- Auditors
- Strategic incident commanders

AI handles:

- Detection
- Prioritization
- Containment

Real-World Early Examples:

- IBM QRadar SOAR
- Google Chronicle
- Palo Alto Cortex XSIAM

11.4 Deep Dive: AI in Offensive Cyber Operations

Future cyberattacks will involve:

Technology	Offensive Application
Generative AI	Create perfect fake emails, voices, even identities
Reinforcement Learning	Optimize malware evasion in real time
Adversarial AI	Attack defender AI models (poison data, confuse detection)
Swarm Intelligence	Distributed malware working cooperatively

Potential Offensive AI Capabilities:

- Self-repairing malware

- Self-cloaking network behaviors
- AI-based exploitation of IoT and edge devices at scale

Defenders must:

- Build **adaptive, dynamic defence models**.
- **Harden** their AI systems against adversarial attacks.

11.5 Emerging Technologies to Master by 2030

Post-Quantum Cryptography
- Lattice-based encryption
- Code-based signatures
- Learning With Errors (LWE) systems

Federated and Privacy-Preserving AI
- Decentralized ML models (without central data gathering)
- Critical for GDPR, HIPAA compliance

Explainable AI (XAI) in Cybersecurity
- AI must explain its decisions (not just black-box output)
- Tools like SHAP, LIME, ELI5 will be fundamental.

Neuro-Symbolic AI
- Combining logic-based reasoning with neural networks.

- Enabling AI to "think" more like humans (with explanations).

Autonomous Deception Systems

- Dynamic honeypots
- Shifting network defences
- Decoy credentials injected by AI

11.6 Career Skills for AI Cybersecurity Professionals (2030+)

Mastery of:

Skill	Why
AI/ML engineering (Python, TensorFlow, PyTorch)	Building and understanding defensive models
Cyber threat intelligence automation	Real-time collection, enrichment, prediction
Cloud-native security	Defending multi-cloud, serverless, container environments
Blockchain and smart contract auditing	Securing decentralized applications
Adversarial machine learning	Defending AI models from attack
Ethical governance and compliance	Implementing safe AI practices

Cybersecurity + AI expertise = one of the most valuable career combinations of the 2030s.

11.7 Final Strategic Advice: Own the Future

To succeed:

- **Learn continuously**: The field will evolve daily.
- **Build practical projects**: Hands-on skills beat theoretical knowledge.
- **Think both offense and defence**: Understand attackers' mindsets.
- **Prioritize ethics**: AI mistakes in cybersecurity can cost real lives.
- **Collaborate**: No one can defend alone — global collaboration is essential.

Chapter 11 Summary

Key Takeaway	Why It Matters
Cybersecurity and AI are converging	The future is autonomous, real-time defence
Prepare now for quantum threats, autonomous SOCs, adversarial AI	Future-proof your skills
Ethical, explainable, privacy-conscious AI is critical	Trust and transparency are security pillars

Those who prepare for 2030 today will **lead the cyber frontiers of tomorrow**.

Chapter 12: Ethical and Legal Challenges Ahead in AI Cybersecurity

12.1 Introduction: Why Ethics and Law Will Define AI Cybersecurity

Artificial intelligence is transforming cybersecurity with unprecedented power.

But with great power comes great responsibility.

**AI-based cybersecurity systems can save systems —
but if misused or left unchecked, they can also harm
human rights, democracy, privacy, and trust.**

The 2025–2030 era demands cybersecurity leaders who:

- Understand **not only technology**
- But also **ethics**, **law**, and **responsible governance**.

This chapter is your **critical guide to future-proofing your
work**.

12.2 The Five Fundamental Ethical Principles for AI Cybersecurity

---

Principle	Explanation
Transparency	Make AI decisions explainable and understandable
Fairness	Ensure AI does not discriminate or create unjust outcomes
Accountability	Humans must remain responsible for AI actions
Privacy	Protect users' data, even when building AI models
Security	Build AI that cannot easily be exploited by attackers

---

Ethical cybersecurity isn't about **being nice** —
it's about **building resilient, trustworthy systems** that
organizations and societies can rely upon.

12.3 Major Ethical Dilemmas in AI Cybersecurity

1. AI Bias and Discrimination

If AI models are trained on biased or incomplete security data:

- They may **over-monitor** certain users or locations.
- They may **miss threats** from groups underrepresented in the training data.

Example:

- SOC AI flagging login attempts from certain IP regions as risky **just based on geography**, not actual behavior.

2. Autonomous Decision-Making and "Kill Chains"

AI systems that autonomously:

- Block users
- Terminate cloud instances
- Delete user accounts
- Shut down business operations

could **cause catastrophic harm** if acting wrongly.

Example:

- False positive anomaly shuts down a hospital's emergency systems.

Thus:

Human oversight must never be fully removed.

3. Adversarial AI and the Risk of AI vs. AI Conflicts

Future:

- Attacker AI learns from defender AI behavior.

- Defender AI adapts to attacker AI's evasion.

If left unchecked, **unsupervised autonomous escalation** could cripple systems unintentionally.

Ethical frameworks must govern:

- How much autonomy defensive AI gets.

- How escalation and shutdown thresholds are enforced.

---

4. Privacy Erosion through Hyper-Collection

Building good AI models often requires:

- Massive user activity datasets.

- Detailed telemetry.

If improperly managed:

- Organizations may violate GDPR, HIPAA, CCPA, or similar laws.

- Individuals' private behaviors could be exposed.

Thus:

Data minimization and **privacy-by-design AI development** are ethical imperatives.

12.4 Legal Landscape for AI in Cybersecurity (2025–2030)

Key emerging legal frameworks to understand:

Regulation	Focus
EU AI Act (passed 2024)	Regulates high-risk AI systems, including cybersecurity tools
GDPR (already enforced)	Data protection, privacy rights
NIS2 Directive (EU)	Cybersecurity requirements for critical infrastructure
U.S. Executive Orders (2025)	Cybersecurity AI accountability, supply chain security
Global Standards (ISO/IEC AI Ethics)	International norms for safe AI practices

Common Legal Requirements Emerging:

- Risk assessments for AI cybersecurity systems.
- Explainability of AI decisions.
- Documentation and audit trails.
- Incident reporting for AI-caused breaches.

Future AI cybersecurity professionals must:

- Collaborate with legal teams.
- Maintain ethical and legal design principles from the **first line of code**.

12.5 Ethical Design Patterns for AI Cybersecurity Systems

Pattern	Purpose
Human-in-the-Loop	Ensure human validation for critical decisions
Model Explainability	Attach reason codes to each AI action
Adversarial Robustness	Harden models against malicious manipulation
Privacy-Preserving ML	Use techniques like differential privacy, federated learning
Ethical Data Collection	Explicit consent, minimal data scope, deletion rights respected

Implement **design patterns** that bake ethics into your AI systems
— not as an afterthought, but as a structural necessity.

12.6 Practical Example: Building Ethical Anomaly Detection AI

Suppose you're building a login anomaly detector.

Ethical steps:

- **Balance training data** to include different geographies, time zones, user types.

- **Explain anomalies**: "Flagged because login occurred at 4AM from unregistered device."

- **Limit scope**: Only monitor data necessary for detection, not full user behavior histories.

Legal steps:

- Obtain **clear consent** for monitoring users' login behavior.

- Provide **opt-out** mechanisms where possible (especially in non-critical environments).

- Maintain **logs of model retraining, validation, and drift correction**.

12.7 Emerging Technologies Supporting Ethical AI Cybersecurity

Technology	Benefit
Federated Learning	Train models across devices without centralizing data
Differential Privacy	Add statistical noise to protect individual records
Homomorphic Encryption	Compute on encrypted data without exposing it
Explainable AI (XAI) Libraries	Interpret and explain model decisions to auditors and regulators

Ethical cybersecurity innovation will **accelerate trust** and give companies competitive advantages — not just regulatory compliance.

12.8 The Future: Global Ethical Cybersecurity Standards

By 2030+, expect:

- International treaties on AI cybersecurity conduct (like cyber "Geneva Conventions").

- Mandatory AI impact assessments for all high-risk digital infrastructure.

- Certifications for ethical AI cybersecurity systems (similar to ISO standards today).

Preparing for this now will:

- Differentiate you as a leader.

- Future-proof your career.

- Help build a more secure, fair, and trusted digital world.

Chapter 12 Summary

Key Takeaway	Why It Matters
AI cybersecurity carries massive ethical responsibility	Protect users, organizations, and societies
Laws are evolving fast	Compliance must be proactive
Ethical design = better security, better trust	Defence without ethics is self-defeating

The **future belongs to cybersecurity leaders** who combine:

- **Technical excellence**

- **Strategic foresight**

- **Ethical courage**

Epilogue: Forging the Next Generation of Cyber Defenders

E.1 Introduction: A Threshold Crossed

As you reach the final pages of this book,
you are no longer the same reader who started this journey.

You are now:

- **Equipped with deep understanding** of AI in cybersecurity.

- **Armed with practical Python skills** to build real-world defensive systems.

- **Strategically aware** of the threats and trends shaping the next decade.

- **Ethically grounded** to lead in a rapidly evolving battlefield.

You are now part of the next generation of cyber defenders.

The torch has passed to those ready not just to react to attacks, but to **anticipate, innovate, and lead** — with wisdom, courage, and mastery.

E.2 The New Battlefield: Mind vs. Machine

The future battlefield is unlike anything the world has ever seen:

Old Cybersecurity	New AI Cybersecurity
Manual incident response	Autonomous, predictive defence systems
Signature-based protection	Behavioral, adaptive, AI-driven models
Human-detected threats	AI-vs-AI conflicts at machine speed
Static systems	Dynamic, evolving cloud-native environments
Reactive strategies	Proactive hunting, self-healing architectures

---

In the future:

- The **first sign of an attack** might be an AI model's statistical anomaly, not a human scream.

- The **first defender** might be an autonomous agent patching a vulnerability in seconds.

- **The first casualty** might be trust — unless ethical, explainable AI stands strong.

E.3 What It Takes to Lead in the 2025–2030 Cybersecurity World

---

Skills Alone Are Not Enough.

To be truly effective, you must embody:

Element	Why It Matters
Technical Mastery	Build and deploy AI systems effectively
Strategic Vision	Predict attacker innovations and defender needs
Ethical Backbone	Maintain trust, legality, and human dignity
Adaptability	Thrive in an environment of perpetual change
Collaborative Spirit	No single defender can secure everything alone

---

The next generation cyber defenders are:

- Coders
- Analysts
- Strategists
- Ethicists
- Leaders

All at once.

E.4 Your Mission: Defence as a Creative Act

Cyber defence is not just a job.
It's a **creative, innovative art**:

- Designing AI that **thinks critically** about anomalies.

- Engineering systems that **adapt faster** than attackers.

- Writing Python code that **transforms raw data into protection**.

- Creating architectures that **predict**, **learn**, **respond**, and **recover** autonomously.

Defence is creation. Defence is innovation. Defence is leadership.

The better you design, the fewer systems fall.
The more creatively you think, the fewer lives are disrupted.

E.5 Building the Future: Practical Steps You Can Take

---

1. Build Real Systems

Start small:

- An anomaly detector for login events.

- A behavioral model for cloud activities.

- A transaction monitor for smart contracts.

Then scale:

- Integrate with real-world platforms.

- Automate detection-to-response workflows.

---

2. Contribute to Open-Source Cybersecurity AI Projects

Help improve:

- AI threat detection engines
- Security automation frameworks
- Adversarial robustness research

Your code could protect thousands, even millions.

---

3. Teach and Mentor

Share your knowledge:

- With junior cybersecurity professionals.
- With cross-functional teams (legal, compliance, operations).

Every defender you uplift multiplies your impact.

---

4. Advocate for Ethical Cybersecurity Practices

Speak up:

- In your workplace.
- In industry forums.
- In policy discussions.

Push for:

- Transparent AI models
- Ethical data collection
- Accountability in automated decisions

---

5. Never Stop Learning

Read:

- New AI research papers.

- Threat reports.
- Legal and regulatory updates.

Build new skills:

- Quantum cybersecurity
- Explainable AI
- Cloud-native security frameworks

The greatest defenders are the most relentless learners.

E.6 Closing Vision: A World Secured by Wisdom, Not Just Code

Imagine a future where:

- **AI protects hospitals** from ransomware before surgeries are delayed.
- **Smart cities stay operational** even under massive cyberattacks.
- **Children's identities are safe** because predictive AI caught threats early.
- **Autonomous vehicles reroute safely** under coordinated cyber defence.
- **Freedom of speech and privacy survive** because cybersecurity professionals stayed ethical, wise, and courageous.

This is not science fiction.

This is the reality you — and your generation — can build.

In cybersecurity, you don't just defend systems.
You defend lives. Futures. Freedoms.

You are needed.

You are capable.

You are ready.

The future is in your hands.

Let's build it — securely, wisely, and boldly.

Appendix A: Best Open Datasets for AI Cybersecurity

A.1 Why Good Datasets Matter

In AI cybersecurity, models are only as good as the data they learn from.

Garbage in = Garbage out.

Access to **high-quality**, **real-world**, and **diverse** datasets is **essential** to:

- Train powerful detection models.
- Test anomaly detection systems.
- Simulate real-world attacks safely.
- Benchmark AI performance fairly.

A.2 Curated List of Top Cybersecurity Datasets

---

1. Canadian Institute for Cybersecurity Datasets (CICIDS series)

- Website: CIC Datasets

- Type: Network traffic, labelled attacks (botnet, DDoS, brute force, web attacks)

- Why Important: Realistic environment simulation with legitimate user activity and attack patterns.

- Famous Versions:

  o CICIDS2017

  o CICIDS2018

  o CSE-CIC-IDS2018

2. UNSW-NB15

- Website: UNSW-NB15 Dataset

- Type: Network flows, various attacks, modern applications

- Why Important: Designed to reflect **modern Internet traffic** and contemporary attacks.

3. CTU-13 Botnet Traffic Dataset

- Website: CTU-13 Dataset

- Type: Botnet network traffic

- Why Important: Specialized for **botnet detection** and anomaly-based defences.

4. DARPA 1998 and 1999 Intrusion Detection Datasets

- Website: DARPA Dataset

- Type: Network captures, various traditional attacks

- Why Important: Historical significance; caution — somewhat outdated but useful for baseline experiments.

---

5. KDDCup99 Dataset (and NSL-KDD Improved Version)

- Website: NSL-KDD

- Type: Connection-level features (network attacks)

- Why Important: Still used in academic benchmarking, but real-world relevance is limited. Prefer newer datasets like CICIDS.

---

6. DAPT 2022 Dataset (Domain Adversarial Penetration Testing)

- Website: DAPT Dataset

- Type: Penetration testing activities simulated on networks

- Why Important: Modern red team vs blue team scenarios for model training.

---

7. VirusShare and MalwareBazaar (Malware Repositories)

- Websites:

  o VirusShare

  o MalwareBazaar

- Type: Malware samples (EXE, binaries, payloads)

- Why Important: Critical for malware classification and behavior analysis projects.

- Warning: Handle malware datasets carefully in secure, isolated environments.

8. DGA (Domain Generation Algorithm) Dataset

- Website: DGArchive Project

- Type: Legitimate vs. DGA-generated domain names

- Why Important: Essential for AI models detecting botnets and domain abuse.

9. Phishing Websites Datasets (PhishTank, UCI)

- Websites:

  - PhishTank

  - UCI Phishing Dataset

- Type: URL-based phishing indicators

- Why Important: Building classifiers for detecting phishing websites and emails.

10. MISP Threat Intelligence Feeds (via Community)

- Website: MISP Project

- Type: Threat intelligence (IP addresses, hashes, URLs, TTPs)

- Why Important: Great for real-world IOC enrichment and TI automation experiments.

A.3 Best Practices When Using Open Datasets

Always:

- Check licensing and permissible usage.

- Understand the **dataset biases** (what attacks, what periods, what traffic types).

- Preprocess carefully: clean anomalies, handle missing values.

- Split into **training / testing** sets properly.

- Simulate **realistic deployment scenarios** — real-world imbalance (e.g., few attacks among lots of benign data).

A.4 Datasets to Be Cautious With

Dataset	Why to be cautious
KDDCup99	Unrealistically high attack ratios, many redundant records
DARPA1998	Outdated protocols and network structures
Random malware samples	Legal and operational risks if mishandled outside safe environments

A.5 Future Datasets Trends (2025+)

Expect more datasets to emerge with:

- Cloud-native telemetry (Kubernetes, serverless functions)

- AI vs. AI adversarial logs

- Blockchain transaction anomalies

- IoT and edge device traffic

Participating in dataset creation (e.g., contributing to open-source security telemetry projects)
is a great way to boost your skills and reputation!

Appendix A Summary

Key Takeaway	Why It Matters
Good datasets = Good models	Better training, better detection, better defence
Understanding biases and structures	Avoid model overfitting and misrepresentation
New data sources are emerging fast	Stay updated to stay effective

The right datasets **train not just your models — but your mind.**

Appendix B: Project Ideas for Aspiring Cyber-AI Builders

B.1 Why Building Projects Matters

Reading builds **knowledge**.
Practicing builds **skills**.
Creating builds **mastery**.

Real-world cybersecurity AI expertise **comes from projects**
—

solving ambiguous, complex problems with your own models
and code.

**You become a true cyber defender not by watching — but
by building.**

B.2 10 High-Impact Cybersecurity AI Project Ideas

Each project idea below includes:

- Concept
- Why It's Important
- Key Python Tools to Use
- Possible Extensions

1. Dynamic Anomaly Detection for Cloud API Logs

Concept:
Build an AI model that monitors cloud API event logs (AWS, Azure, GCP) and flags anomalous usage patterns.

Why Important:
Attackers exploit cloud misconfigurations faster than traditional environments.

Tools:
Pandas, Scikit-Learn, Isolation Forest, AWS Boto3, Google API Python Client

Extensions:
Integrate with Slack or email alerts for real-time SOC notifications.

---

2. AI-Powered Smart Contract Vulnerability Predictor

Concept:
Create an AI tool that parses Solidity code (Ethereum smart contracts) and predicts if vulnerabilities are likely.

Why Important:
Smart contract bugs have already caused multi-billion dollar losses.

Tools:
Python AST, TensorFlow/Keras, Solidity code parsers (like Mythril)

Extensions:
Develop a browser plugin that warns users before interacting with risky contracts.

---

3. Phishing Website Detector Using Machine Learning

Concept:
Train a classifier that distinguishes between phishing and legitimate websites based on URL and metadata features.

Why Important:
Phishing remains the #1 initial attack vector worldwide.

Tools:
Scikit-Learn, XGBoost, BeautifulSoup, Whois libraries

Extensions:
Build a Chrome extension that warns users in real-time.

---

4. Behavioral Biometrics Anomaly Detector

Concept:
Create an AI system that monitors typing speed, mouse movement, and click patterns to detect account hijacking.

Why Important:
Credential theft bypasses traditional password defences.

Tools:
Pandas, Keras/TensorFlow, behavioral tracking libraries (e.g., PyAutoGUI)

Extensions:
Multi-device models (desktop, mobile) for user behavior profiles.

---

5. Autonomous Threat Intelligence Collector and Enricher

Concept:
Scrape threat intelligence feeds, enrich IOCs automatically with WHOIS, VirusTotal, and Shodan data.

Why Important:
Manual TI analysis is too slow in the AI-driven cyberwar era.

Tools:
Requests, Shodan API, VirusTotal API, MISP integration, NLP for parsing TI blogs

Extensions:
Auto-generate daily threat intelligence reports for security teams.

---

6. AI-Driven Ransomware Behavior Predictor

Concept:
Build a model that predicts whether a running process exhibits ransomware behavior based on system calls.

Why Important:
Early ransomware detection could save organizations millions.

Tools:
Sysmon logs, Pandas, LightGBM, EDR telemetry simulation

Extensions:
Real-time kill switch integrated into endpoint security agents.

---

7. IoT Device Fingerprinting and Anomaly Detection

Concept:
Train a model that profiles normal IoT device behavior (network traffic, packet size, frequency) and flags anomalies.

Why Important:
IoT devices are notoriously insecure and difficult to monitor at scale.

Tools:
Scapy, NetworkX, PyShark, Isolation Forest, KMeans Clustering

Extensions:
Edge-deployed versions for routers and small gateways.

---

8. Blockchain Transaction Fraud Detector

Concept:
Analyse blockchain transaction graphs to detect anomalous transaction flows suggesting laundering or fraud.

Why Important:
Crypto finance systems are high-value targets for fraud.

Tools:
NetworkX, PyTorch Geometric (graph neural networks), APIs from Etherscan or Blockchain.info

Extensions:
Score-risk-based wallet reputation system.

---

9. AI-Assisted Malware Family Classifier

Concept:
Use machine learning to classify malware binaries into families based on their binary features or disassembled code.

Why Important:
Fast classification speeds up incident response dramatically.

Tools:
Pandas, LightGBM, Feature hashing, PEfile (Windows Portable Executable analysis)

Extensions:
Feed models into SOAR workflows for dynamic triage.

---

10. Explainable AI Framework for Security Analysts

Concept:
Build an interface that explains to analysts why a specific security alert was generated by an AI model.

Why Important:
Trust in AI cybersecurity requires explainability — especially under new laws (e.g., EU AI Act).

Tools:
SHAP, LIME, Streamlit for dashboarding

Extensions:
Tie explanations into analyst playbooks for better alert investigation.

B.3 How to Succeed with These Projects

Start small: Build a working prototype first.
Iterate fast: Add features incrementally (MVP mindset).
Document your work: Critical for demonstrating skills to employers or collaborators.
Open-source if possible: Contributing public code boosts visibility and credibility.

Each project you complete becomes a stepping stone toward cybersecurity mastery.

Appendix B Summary

Key Takeaway	Why It Matters
Projects solidify knowledge into skills	Practical application is essential for cybersecurity AI
Python + AI + Security = Unbeatable combination	Skillsets aligned with 2025–2030 demand
Think creatively and iterate	Cyber defence innovation never ends

Your next mission: **Choose a project. Start today. Build the future.**

Appendix C: Further Python Tools and Libraries You Must Know for AI Cybersecurity

C.1 Introduction: Beyond the Basics

You've already learned core libraries (like Scikit-learn, TensorFlow, Pandas, Matplotlib).
But the world of **Python for AI cybersecurity** is much deeper and richer.

Advanced defenders master **specialized tools** that make building, scaling, and securing AI systems faster and smarter.

This appendix introduces **the next tier of powerful Python resources**
— essential for real-world deployment at scale in 2025–2030.

C.2 Specialized Libraries for Advanced AI Cybersecurity

1. PyOD — Python Outlier Detection

- Description: Comprehensive toolkit for detecting outlying objects and novel events.

- Use Cases: Behavioral anomaly detection, fraud detection, intrusion detection.

- Features:
    - Over 30 detection algorithms (kNN, Isolation Forest, AutoEncoders, HBOS)
    - Easy to integrate with Scikit-learn pipelines.

Example:

from pyod.models.iforest import IForest

from pyod.utils.data import generate_data

X_train, X_test, y_train, y_test = generate_data(n_train=200, n_test=100, n_features=2)

clf = IForest()

clf.fit(X_train)

y_test_pred = clf.predict(X_test)

Ideal for building sophisticated anomaly detection pipelines quickly!

2. Adversarial Robustness Toolbox (ART)

- Description: Open-source library by IBM to defend ML models against adversarial threats.

- Use Cases: Model hardening, adversarial attack simulation.

Features:

- Attacks: FGSM, DeepFool, Carlini-Wagner
- Defences: Adversarial training, defensive distillation

Example:

from art.attacks.evasion import FastGradientMethod

from art.estimators.classification import SklearnClassifier

Wrap your sklearn model

classifier = SklearnClassifier(model=your_model)

attack = FastGradientMethod(estimator=classifier, eps=0.2)

x_test_adv = attack.generate(x=x_test)

 Critical for preparing AI models to survive sophisticated attack attempts.

---

3. PyCaret

- Description: Low-code machine learning library.
- Use Cases: Fast prototyping of ML models in cybersecurity (especially SOC automations).

Features:

- Auto-preprocessing
- Model comparison
- Automated hyperparameter tuning

Example:

from pycaret.classification import *

exp = setup(data=df, target='is_anomaly')

best_model = compare_models()

Perfect for rapid deployment of proof-of-concept detection systems!

---

4. Scapy

- Description: Packet crafting, sniffing, and analysis library.
- Use Cases: Network traffic analysis, custom packet-based attack detection, honeypot development.

Features:

- Generate custom packets
- Sniff live network traffic
- Modify TCP/IP stack behaviors

Example:

from scapy.all import *

```
def monitor_packets(pkt):
    if pkt.haslayer(TCP) and pkt[TCP].dport == 22:
        print(f"SSH packet detected from {pkt[IP].src}")


sniff(prn=monitor_packets, filter="tcp", store=0)
```

Essential for any AI system that operates on raw network telemetry.

---

5. Faker

- Description: Python library for generating fake datasets.
- Use Cases: Simulating security events (login logs, access patterns) for model training and validation.

Example:

from faker import Faker

fake = Faker()

print(fake.ipv4(), fake.user_name(), fake.date_time_this_year())

Great for creating large training datasets when real-world data isn't available yet.

C.3 Useful NLP Libraries for Threat Intelligence

Library	Use Case
spaCy	Named entity recognition, fast NLP pipelines
HuggingFace Transformers	Large Language Models (LLMs) for summarizing reports
nltk	Traditional NLP (tokenization, stemming, POS tagging)

Example:

- Parse phishing emails.

- Summarize threat intelligence articles.

- Extract IoCs automatically.

C.4 Frameworks for Scaling AI Cybersecurity Projects

Framework	Why It Matters
TensorFlow Extended (TFX)	Production-grade ML pipeline management
MLflow	Track experiments, model deployments, version control
Kubernetes + Kubeflow	Deploy scalable AI cybersecurity models across clusters
FastAPI	Create APIs to serve AI models securely

AI cybersecurity is not just modelling — it's operationalization.

C.5 Real-World Tips for Using Advanced Libraries

Best Practices:

- **Always isolate environments** (use venvs or Docker containers).

- **Optimize models for production** (quantization, pruning if needed).

- **Secure data pipelines** (authentication, authorization, encryption).

- **Document experiments** (using MLflow, spreadsheets, or GitHub repos).

Ethical Note:

- If working with real user data, ensure full compliance with GDPR, HIPAA, or local privacy laws.

- Never retain personally identifiable information (PII) unnecessarily.

Appendix C Summary

Key Takeaway	Why It Matters
Specialized tools unlock advanced projects	Handle complex, large-scale cybersecurity use cases
Master operational pipelines	Real systems go beyond just model training
Continue expanding your tech stack	2025–2030 cybersecurity demands breadth and depth

Mastering these advanced Python tools **equips you to build world-class cybersecurity AI systems** — ready for the fierce future ahead.

Further Reading and Resources

Why Further Learning Matters

Cybersecurity and AI are dynamic fields.

The skills and knowledge you've gained from this book will serve as your foundation —
but the **threat landscape, technology stack, and legal framework** will keep evolving rapidly through 2025, 2030, and beyond.

Lifelong learning is essential.

The best defenders are always students.

Here are curated further reading materials, courses, and references to continue mastering AI cybersecurity.

Recommended Books

Title	Why It's Important
"Artificial Intelligence for Cybersecurity" by Mark Stamp	Deep technical explanation of how AI models intersect with cybersecurity
"Machine Learning for Cybersecurity Cookbook" by Emmanuel Tsukerman	Practical recipes for building ML-based security systems
"Hands-On Machine Learning with Scikit-Learn, Keras, and TensorFlow" by Aurélien Géron	Comprehensive guide for modern ML workflows
"Cybersecurity and Cyberwar: What Everyone Needs to Know" by P.W. Singer and Allan Friedman	Strategic context behind technical defences

Title	Why It's Important
"Trustworthy AI" by Beena Ammanath	Ethics and governance considerations in building AI systems

Must-Follow Research Papers and Reports

Source	Why Follow
MIT Lincoln Laboratory AI and Cybersecurity Research	Cutting-edge AI applications in security
Google DeepMind's AI Safety Research	How to build safe, ethical AI
Microsoft Security Blog (AI and Cyber Threats Focus)	Early threat detections and defence strategies
ENISA Threat Landscape Reports	Europe's official cybersecurity threat analyses
IBM X-Force Threat Intelligence Index	Annual real-world attack trends and emerging AI threats

Online Courses and Certifications

Platform	Course
Coursera	"AI for Everyone" by Andrew Ng (general AI mindset)

Platform	Course
edX (Linux Foundation)	"AI for Cybersecurity"
Udemy	"Cybersecurity Data Science: Machine Learning for Cyber Threat Detection"
Cybrary	"AI and Machine Learning for Cybersecurity"
Stanford Online	"CS229: Machine Learning" (for deeper math and algorithms)

Many major cloud providers (AWS, Azure, GCP) also offer **ML + Security** specialization tracks.
Highly recommended for practical enterprise work!

Practical Tools and Communities

Resource	Purpose
OWASP Machine Learning Security Top 10	Understanding threats to ML systems
ThreatOps Slack / Discord Communities	Connect with cybersecurity researchers and practitioners
Open Threat Research (OTR) Community	Access to open-source threat hunting datasets and projects
DEFCON AI Village Talks	Future of adversarial AI, offensive security research

Stay **connected** to **communities** — they often hear about vulnerabilities, innovations, and attacks **first**, before the mainstream.

Final Advice on Continuing Education

Always keep a **"learning sprint" journal**:

- Every week, tackle one paper, one article, or one small project.
- Record what you learned, what you tried, what failed, and what worked.

Mix **theory** (research, papers) and **practice** (coding, modelling).

Attend **cybersecurity AI competitions**, like Kaggle challenges or CTFs (Capture The Flag competitions) with an AI twist.

Set **impossible goals** for yourself:

- Build an AI system that no one has built yet.
- Detect threats others miss.
- Predict the future before it happens.

The future of cybersecurity belongs to those who never stop pushing forward.

About the Author

Education:

- Doctor of Science (DSc) in Project Evaluation, Technion, Haifa, Israel
- Master of Science (MSc) in Operations Research, London School of Economics
- Bachelor of Science (BSc) in Industrial and Management Engineering, Technion, Haifa, Israel

Teaching and Academic Research Positions Held:

- Micro Economics
- Macro Economics
- Econometrics
- Statistics
- Mathematics
- Public Finance
- Urban Planning Mathematical Models
- Transportation Science

Urban and Regional Planning Experience:

- Comprehensive Urban Renewal Project Manager (Physical and Social Project) of the East Acco Government Project. Received the title Yakir Acco from the Acco municipality.

Mathematical Modelling Projects:

- Optimal production mix model using linear programming for the Israeli Paper Mill, Hedera.
- Optimal loading and unloading of ships in Ashdod port using mathematical simulation and integer programming models for the Phosphates at the Negev company.
- Optimal mining order for the Phosphates at the Negev company using mathematical linear, integer, and nonlinear programming.
- Optimal ship operation to transport crude oil using a simulation model for the Institute of By Sea Transport at Haifa.
- Traffic assignment mathematical model for the Transportation Science Institute, Technion, Haifa.
- Industrial Land use analysis in the city of Tel Aviv using Principal Factors Analysis for Tel Aviv Municipality.
- Pupils distribution among the Tel Aviv school system using an integer programming model for the Municipality of Tel Aviv.
- Various mathematical programming models for El Al, The Electric Company, Teva, etc., in association with the Representative of SAS in Israel (Maia Computers).

- Truck fleet routing model based on mathematical programming and heuristics models for international clientele.
- Optimal Locomotive and personnel assignment (run cutting problem) to trains using integer programming models for the New York City Transit Authority.
- Statistical analysis for sales for the American Cyanamid company in Pearl River, New Jersey.
- Sales analysis models (econometric and statistical models) for JC Penny, USA.

Professional Experience:

- Founding partner (2006-2011) in the company "Kaul and Lomovasky Holdings Inc" specializing in the computerization of trading using artificial intelligence.
- Internet and Artificial Intelligence Programmer, Developer, and Consultant (2012-2018).
- Developed an AI-based system to calculate the price of apartments in 300 towns in Israel, using VBA Excel Neural Networks (artificial intelligence) pre-processing and presented the prices on a Python Django-based website.
- Author of several books on topics such as Futurology, Python, algorithmic trading, quantum computing, crypto trading, artificial intelligence, Urbanism, Economics, Public Policy, Operations Research, Tariffs and Trade Wars and startup ideas.

Computer Programming Skills:

- C, VBA under Excel, Microsoft Office, HTML, PHP, MATLAB, SAS, Python, Django, Keras, Panda, Cloud AI

Applications, TensorFlow, Google Cloud Platform, OpenCV, Adversarial GANs, Computer Vision, Image Classification, Object Recognition, Pose Recognition.

- Quantum computing and quantum machine learning. Algorithm development, end-to-end ownership.

Related Publications (2018-2025)

-Python for Non-Programmers: Building Your AI, App, and Automation Projects from Scratch: Your Complete Beginner's Guide to Python, Automation, and AI-Powered Web Apps Kindle Edition

by Dr Israel Carlos Lomovasky (Author) Format: Kindle Edition

-Algorithmic Trading with Python Amid Tariffs and Trade Wars: Foundations to AI Strategies (The 2025–2030 Manual): Beginners Friendly. Python Code Explained ... Discussed Thoroughly (Economic Turbulence) Kindle Edition

by Dr Israel Carlos Lomovasky (Author) Format: Kindle Edition

-Tariffs, Trade Wars and the Magnificent Seven Stocks: Trading and Investing 2025–2030: Apple, Microsoft, Alphabet, Amazon, Meta, Nvidia and Tesla. (Economic Turbulence) Kindle Edition

by Dr Israel Carlos Lomovasky (Author) Format: Kindle Edition

-Navigating Trade Wars and Technological Shifts: 12 Startup Opportunities (2025–2027): Turning Tariff Tensions into Breakthrough Startup Models Based on Cutting Edge High Tech (Economic Turbulence) Kindle Edition

by Dr Israel Carlos Lomovasky (Author) Format: Kindle Edition

-US–China Trade War: Current Status, Scenarios, and Investment Strategy (2025 – 2026): Turn the turbulence of geopolitical tension into your next investment advantage Kindle Edition

by Dr Israel Carlos Lomovasky (Author) Format: Kindle Edition

-Day Trading Equities, ETFs, Options, Futures , Amid Global Trade Wars and Tariffs (2025 Report): Beginners to Advanced. Real Time Strategies and Examples. Global and US Markets (Economic Turbulence) Kindle Edition

by Dr Israel Carlos Lomovasky (Author) Format: Kindle Edition

-Safeguard and Prosper: Mastering Portfolio Strategy Amid Tariffs and Trade Wars. Portfolio Protecting Briefing 2025: Is your Investment Portfolio Ready ... and Tariff Turbulence (Economic Turbulence) Kindle Edition

by Dr Israel Carlos Lomovasky (Author) Format: Kindle Edition

-Making Money Under Tariffs and Trade Wars. Business Ideas Briefing: Strategies like Import Substitution, Reshoring Partnerships, Tariff Arbitrage, and Specialized Consulting (Economic Turbulence) Kindle Edition

by Dr Israel Carlos Lomovasky (Author) Format: Kindle Edition

-Tariffs and the Stock Market: Trading and Investing in a Turbulent Economy: The Knowledge you (Seasoned or Beginner) Need, to Trade and Invest Profitably in These Tumultuous Times. Kindle Edition

by Dr Israel Carlos Lomovasky (Author) Format: Kindle Edition

- Navigating the Storm: A Comprehensive Guide to Thriving Amid Trade Wars and Tariff Uncertainty: Practical Strategies for Citizens, Businesses, Governments ... and Prosper Globally (Economic Turbulence) Kindle Edition

by Dr Israel Carlos Lomovasky (Author) Format: Kindle Edition

-One World, One Future: Overcoming National Divisions Through Global Governance and Decentralized Democracy: A Visionary Blueprint :a Planet-Wide Government ... Minds Social Direct Democracy (MOTMSDD)) Kindle Edition

by Dr Israel Carlos Lomovasky (Author) Format: Kindle Edition

-AI for Business: Strategies for Non-Technical Managers: Comprehensive yet Digestible, Practical Advice, Real-World Success Stories, Future insights- a ... learning-Python Book 5) Kindle Edition

by Dr Israel Carlos Lomovasky (Author) Format: Kindle Edition

-The Journey to Humanity's Far Future : Crucial Questions that Need to be Explored Pushing the Edge of Imagination: State of the Art Ongoing Futurology ... - Futurology - Futurism - Science Fiction) Kindle Edition

by Dr Israel Carlos Lomovasky (Author) Format: Kindle Edition

-Future Foundations: A Beginner's Guide to Futurology for Business, Government, and Beyond: Your Complete Roadmap to Exploring and Shaping Tomorrow's World! (Futures sciences - Futurology - Futurism) Kindle Edition

by Dr Israel Carlos Lomovasky (Author) Format: Kindle Edition

-The Future of Conflict Resolution: Harnessing Technology and Human-Centered Approaches: AI, Hybrid AI-Human, Blockchain, BCI, Neuroscience, Virtual Reality, MOTMSDD, Quantum, Restorative Justice Kindle Edition

by Dr Israel Carlos Lomovasky (Author) Format: Kindle Edition

-AutoML Meets Real Estate: A No-Code Approach to Property Tech Innovation: Comprehensive ,Beginner-Friendly, with Step-by-Step Guidance for Real-World PropTech Projects. Kindle Edition

by Dr Israel Carlos lomovasky (Author) Format: Kindle Edition

-The AutoML Edge: Creating High-Performance Trading Algorithms Without Coding: AutoML Democratizes Algorithmic Trading, Enabling Traders to Leverage the Power of Machine Learning without Writing Code Kindle Edition

by Dr Israel Carlos Lomovasky (Author) Format: Kindle Edition

-AI Made Simple: How AutoML is Changing Business Without Coding: No Code, Low Code, Practical, Beginners to Advanced, Marketing, Finance, Healthcare, Retail, ... learning-Python Book 4) Kindle Edition

by Dr Israel Carlos Lomovasky (Author) Format: Kindle Edition

-Minds, Machines, and the Metropolis: How MOTMSDD, AI, and IoT Will Reimagine Urban Life: Future of Urbanism with Metaverse of the Minds Social Direct Democracy ... & Cutting Edge, Sustainable Technologies Kindle Edition

by Dr Israel Carlos Lomovasky (Author) Format: Kindle Edition

-The Profitable Algorithmic Trading Manual with AI/ML and Python for Beginners to Advanced: Retail & Institutional. Stocks, ETFs, Forex, Crypto, Options, More. Developing, Deploying & Scaling Kindle Edition

by Dr Israel Carlos Lomovasky (Author) Format: Kindle Edition

-PropTech Innovation with Python: A Complete Step-by-Step Guide with Applied Real Estate Code Examples: Real Estate Revolution: Encyclopedic PropTech Solutions with Python, Foundations to Advanced Kindle Edition

by Dr Israel Carlos Lomovasky (Author) Format: Kindle Edition

-PropTech (Property Technology): Analysing the Impact of Technology on Real Estate Finance.: Blockchain, Smart Contracts, AI/ML in Property Management. Smart Buildings & Virtual and Augmented Reality Kindle Edition

by Dr Israel Carlos lomovasky (Author) Format: Kindle Edition

-Democracy Reimagined: Exposing Populism and Charting a Path to a True Democratic Revival: Populism Unveiled: Democratic Innovations for a Resilient Future ... Minds Social Direct Democracy (MOTMSDD)) Kindle Edition

by Dr Israel Carlos Lomovasky (Author) Format: Kindle Edition

-Crypto Market Mechanics: A New Playbook for Investors and Traders: Crypto Specific: Economics, Correlations, Global Events, Psychology, Risk, Diversification, ... AI Algos, Technical Analysis & Indicators Kindle Edition
by Dr Israel Carlos Lomovasky (Author) Format: Kindle Edition

-Crypto for Beginners: A Step-by-Step Guide to Digital Currency Investing and Trading: Comprehensive and Detailed Guide to Cryptocurrency Investing, Including ... the Blockchain Industry (FINANCE Book 11) Kindle Edition
by Dr Israel Carlos Lomovasky (Author) Format: Kindle Edition

Book 8 of 8: FINANCE

-Quantum Wealth: Mastering Investments in the Quantum Computing Boom.: Quantum Opportunities: Investing in Breakthrough Technologies. Foundations to Advanced. Kindle Edition
by Dr Israel Carlos Lomovasky (Author) Format: Kindle Edition

-AI Investment Mastery: How to Outperform the Market with AI Assets: Comprehensive. Investing in AI Stocks, ETFs, Mutual Funds, Venture Capital, Private ... Foundations to Advanced (FINANCE Book 9) Kindle Edition
by Dr Israel Carlos Lomovasky (Author) Format: Kindle Edition

Book 8 of 8: FINANCE

-The Quantum Nexus: AI, Blockchain, and the Future of Everything: How these Cutting-edge Technologies will Converge to Reshape Various Industries and Everyday ... - Futurology - Science fiction Book 8) Kindle Edition
by Dr Israel Carlos Lomovasky (Author) Format: Kindle Edition

-Coding the Citizen's Voice: Python Tools for MOTMSDD in Governance and Planning: the Manual: Python Source Code. AI & Data Science. Metaverse of the Minds ... and Brain Computer Interface Book 9) Kindle Edition
by Dr Israel Carlos Lomovasky (Author) Format: Kindle Edition

Book 8 of 8: The future implications of the combination between the Internet, the Metaverse and Brain Computer Interface

-Beyond the Vote: AI Applications in Direct Democracy and Civic Engagement: Integrating AI, ML, NLP, Data Visualization, and MOTMSDD Into Public Governance ... and Brain Computer Interface Book 8) Kindle Edition
by Dr Israel Carlos Lomovasky (Author) Format: Kindle Edition

Beyond Quantum: The Next Leap in Computational Paradigms: Exploring the Future of Advanced Computing Technologies (Quantum Computing Book 5) Kindle Edition
by Dr Israel Carlos Lomovasky (Author) Format: Kindle Edition

Book 5 of 5: Quantum Computing

-AI-Proof Your Career: Building Resilience in the Face of Automation: Strategies for Healthcare,Finance,Manufacturing,Art,Entertainment,Retail,Transportation,Energy,Logistics,Government,Teaching Kindle Edition
by Dr Israel Carlos Lomovasky (Author) Format: Kindle Edition

-Defensive Trading in Crypto ETFs: Protecting Your Portfolio in Volatile Markets: The Damage and Losses Control Bible for The Crypto ETFs Investor and Trader Kindle Edition
by Dr Israel Carlos Lomovasky (Author) Format: Kindle Edition

-Algorithmic Trading for Everyone: A Non-Programmer's Journey to Automation: Comprehensive Introduction to Algo Trading for Beginners Without Programming Background Kindle Edition
by Dr Israel Carlos Lomovasky (Author) Format: Kindle Edition

Book 10 of 10: TRADING

-The Great Crypto Illusion: Navigating the Future of Valueless Assets : Examining the Sustainability of Cryptocurrencies Without Traditional Intrinsic Value. (FINANCE Book 8) Kindle Edition
by Dr Israel Carlos Lomovasky (Author) Format: Kindle Edition

-Navigating Crypto ETFs Trading: An Absolute Beginners Guide to New Markets: Foundations of Crypto ETF Trading: Building Your Digital Investment Portfolio Kindle Edition
by Dr Israel Carlos Lomovasky (Author) Format: Kindle Edition
-Profit and Protect: Retail Trading Strategies to Manage Risk and Grow Your Wealth: Foundations to Advanced. Stocks, Bonds, Crypto, Commodities & Forex. Hedging with Options, Swaps, Futures & More Kindle Edition
by Dr Israel Carlos Lomovasky (Author) Format: Kindle Edition

-The Future Game: Unleashing AI and Quantum Computing Power in Game Theory.: Beginners to Advanced.Python Code.Case studies:Economics,Finance,Politics,Environment,Social Science,Psychology,Health,More Kindle Edition
By Dr Israel Carlos Lomovasky (Author) Format: Kindle Edition

-AI and Quantum Strategies: Python's Role in Economic Innovation: Foundations to Advanced. With python and Quantum Code in a Computational Economics Range of Case Studies Kindle Edition
by Dr Israel Carlos Lomovasky (Author) Format: Kindle Edition

-Quantum Computing in Finance: Bridging Theory and Practice with Python: Case Studies: Algorithmic Trading, Risk Management, Fraud Detection, Options Pricing ,Economic Forecasting and more
by Dr Israel Carlos Lomovasky (Author)

Book 6 of 6: FINANCE

-Artificial Gods: The Onset of Superior Machine Intelligence and Consciousness: : The Why and How of a Ban on Research Leading To Superintelligence And AI Consciousness Kindle Edition
by Dr Israel Carlos Lomovasky (Author)

-Quantum and Consciousness: Exploring the Mind-Computer Interface: Unveiling the Quantum Mind: Quantum Computing and the Fabric of Consciousness Kindle Edition
by Dr Israel Carlos Lomovasky (Author)

-Quantum Democracy: Unleashing MOTMSDD with Quantum Computing: MOTMSDD : Metaverse Of The Minds Social Direct Democracy (The future implications of the ... and Brain Computer Interface Book 6) Kindle Edition
by Dr Israel Carlos Lomovasky (Author)

-MOTMSDD: Metaverse Of The Minds Social Direct Democracy: Governance and Public Decision Making in The Era of Brain Computer Interface, AI and Metaverse, ... and Brain Computer Interface Book 5) Kindle Edition
by Dr Israel Carlos Lomovasky (Author)

-MOTMSDD Urbanism:Redefining Cities through AI and
Metaverse of the Minds Social Direct Democracy: Sustainable
Urbanism in the Age of Brain-Computer Interface.Solving
Conflicts between Citizen's Needs Kindle Edition
by Dr Israel Carlos Lomovasky (Author)

-AI in Financial Markets: A Guide to Algorithmic Trading with
ChatGPT: Python Code. CHATGPT Assistance. Basics to
Advanced. Traditional and AI/ML Trading. (FINANCE Book
6) Kindle Edition
by Dr Israel Carlos Lomovasky (Author)

-Python for Financial Freedom: Algorithmic Strategies for
Personal Wealth: Trading and Investing. Foundations to
Advanced. AI/ML, Risk ,Tax ,and Money Management. Stocks
& Crypto (FINANCE Book 5) Kindle Edition
by Dr Israel Carlos Lomovasky (Author)

-Quantum Foundations of Computer Vision: A Guide for
Researchers and Practitioners: Python and Quantum
Language Code. Future Proof Computer Vision (Quantum
Computing Book 3) Kindle Edition
by Dr Israel Carlos Lomovasky (Author)

-MOTMSDD ECONOMICS: From Classical Economics, to
Metaverse Of The Minds Social Direct Democracy
Economics.: For The Next WELFARE ECONOMICS:
Harnessing BCI ... the Metaverse . (FUTURE ECONOMICS
Book 1) Kindle Edition
by Dr Israel Carlos Lomovasky (Author)

-Quantum Hedge: Unlocking the Future of Algorithmic
Trading. : Python and Quantum Languages Code. Basics to
Advanced. Stocks, Forex and Crypto. Theory and Hands on
Practice. Kindle Edition
by Dr Israel Carlos Lomovasky (Author)

-Quantum Economics: Rethinking Macro and Micro in the Age of Quantum Computing: Theory and Practice: Python and Quantum Language Code Explained Step by Step (FUTURE ECONOMICS Book 2) Kindle Edition
by Dr Israel Carlos Lomovasky (Author)

-Driving with the Mind: Exploring MOTMSDD and Its Impact on Smart Cities and Autonomous Mobility: MOTMSDD: Metaverse of The Minds Social Direct Democracy: ... Meets The Metaverse (URBANISM Book 4) Kindle Edition
by Dr Israel Carlos Lomovasky (Author)

-AI in Fundamental Analysis: Uncovering Hidden Algorithmic Investment Opportunities with Python.: Machine,Reinforcement and Deep Learning.Complete AI-Driven ... Advanced.Risk Management. (FINANCE Book 2) Kindle Edition
by Dr Israel Carlos Lomovasky (Author)

-Python for AI and Creativity: Unleashing the Power of Artificial Intelligence in the Arts: Basics to Advanced.Visual Arts,Design,Music,Poetry,Storytelling, ... learning-Python Book 3) Kindle Edition
by Dr Israel Carlos Lomovasky (Author)

-Python for Machine Learning. From Intermediate to Advanced Guide With Code.: Unleash the Potential of Advanced Machine Learning in Python. Covering Many ... learning-Python Book 2) Kindle Edition
by Dr Israel Carlos Lomovasky (Author)

-Python for Smart Cities: Machine Learning and Artificial Intelligence Applications for Urban Planning and Infrastructure: Python in Action: ML/AI for Smart ... Infrastructure Management (URBANISM Book 2) Kindle Edition
by Dr Israel Carlos Lomovasky (Author)

-Python for Machine Learning: A Beginner's Guide.From Scratch to intermediate.: Basis For Algorithmic Finance, Trading, Healthcare, Industry, Transportation, ... learning-Python Book 1) Kindle Edition
by Dr Israel Carlos Lomovasky (Author)

-SINGULARITY'S VEIL: THE RISE AND FALL OF HUMANITY. : A TALE BETWEEN SCIENCE FICTION AND FUTUROLOGY. STOP ARTIFICIAL GENERAL INTELLIGENCE NOW. (Future sciences - Futurology - Science fiction Book 6) Kindle Edition
by Dr Israel Carlos Lomovasky (Author)
-KILLING THE BEAST. THE THREAT OF ADVANCING ARTIFICIAL GENERAL INTELLIGENCE.: A CALL TO BAN AGI.SURVIVAL OF HUMANITY ON THE LINE. A CONTRARIAN NARRATIVE ... - Futurology - Science fiction Book 5) Kindle Edition
by Dr Israel Carlos Lomovasky (Author)

-Day Trading Basics to Advanced:A Comprehensive Guide.From Scalping to AI/ML.Algorithmic Trading.Python Code.: Day Trading Decoded:Unlocking Secrets to Profitable Trading.Stocks,Crypto,Options,Forex Kindle Edition
by Dr Israel Carlos Lomovasky (Author)

-BEGINNER'S MACHINE LEARNING AND ARTIFICIAL INTELLIGENCE IN PYTHON FOR FINANCE: A GUIDE.: EXPLORING THE INTERSECTION OF FINANCE AND ML/AI: A PYTHON PRIMER Kindle Edition
by Dr Israel Carlos Lomovasky (Author)

-The Internet Of Minds (IOM). An Essay: The Future Implications of Brain Computer Interface
by Dr Israel Carlos Lomovasky (Author)

-CRYPTO TRADING TECHNICAL ANALYSIS: Apply the technical analysis indicators, time-frames and approaches that fit Crypto Currencies trading characteristics. Kindle Edition
by Dr Israel Carlos Lomovasky (Author)

-QUANTUM MACHINE LEARNING: A COMPREHENSIVE GUIDE WITH PRACTICAL EXAMPLES AND QUANTUM LANGUAGE IMPLEMENTATION: FROM BASICS TO ADVANCED.INCLUDES PYTHON CODE. (Quantum Computing Book 2) Kindle Edition
by Dr Israel Carlos Lomovasky (Author)

-CRYPTO BASICS TO ADVANCED. MAKE MONEY WITH CRYPTO.THE CRYPTO BUSINESS STARTUP BIBLE.: Investing ,trading and beyond. 20 Cryptocurrency profitable strategies. Over 100 startup ideas. Kindle Edition
by Dr Israel Carlos Lomovasky (Author)

-QUANTUM COMPUTING AND OPERATIONS RESEARCH.AN ESSAY.WHAT IS QC AND WHY IT MATTERS TO OR PRACTITIONERS.: THE FUTURE IMPLICATIONS OF QUANTUM COMPUTING ON OPTIMIZATION AND OPERATIONS RESEARCH. Kindle Edition
by Dr Israel Carlos Lomovasky (Author)

-ALGORITHMIC TRADING FROM SCRATCH TO AI/ML STRATEGIES IMPLEMENTED IN PYTHON.FOR CRYPTO,STOCKS,FOREX AND MORE.: RETAIL TRADING SYSTEMS FROM BASIC TO SOPHISTICATED STEP BY STEP. PYTHON FOR YOUR PROJECTS. Paperback – May 17, 2023
by Dr Israel Carlos Lomovasky (Author)

-CRYPTO SENTIMENT ALGO TRADING.PYTHON AND PSEUDO-CODE.: Algo Cryptocurrencies Trade: day, trend, news, swing, arbitrage, bots, contrarian, volume, event, seasonal ,and more strategies. Kindle Edition
by Dr Israel Carlos Lomovasky (Author)

-

www.ingramcontent.com/pod-product-compliance
Lightning Source LLC
LaVergne TN
LVHW022344060326
832902LV00022B/4242